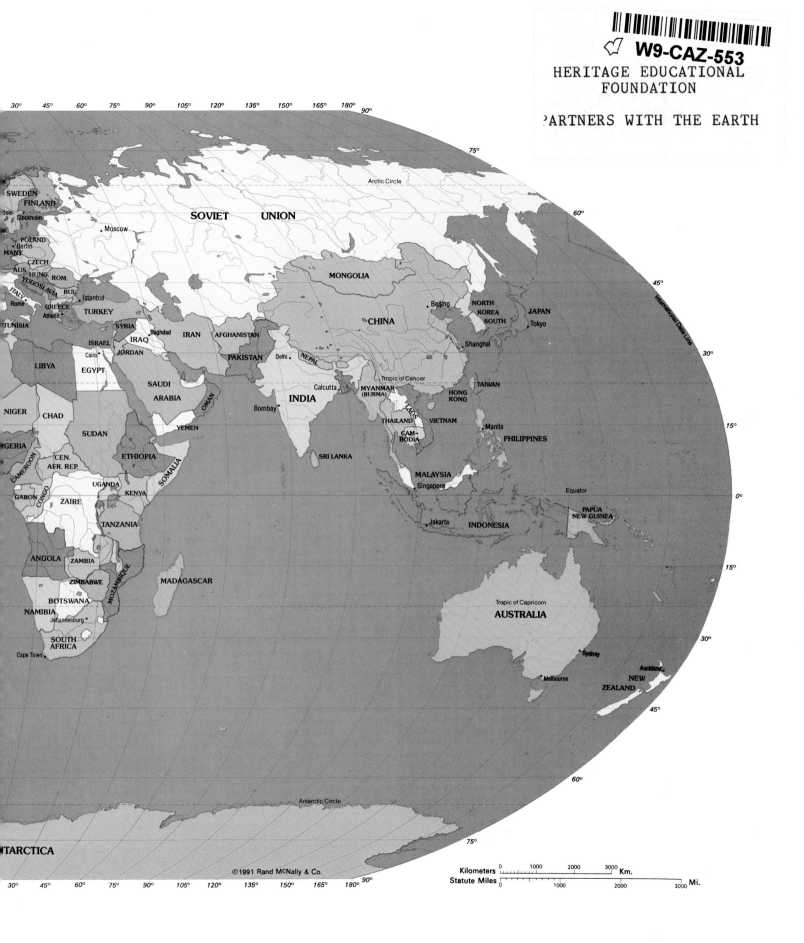

W9-CAZ-553
HERITAGE EDUCATIONAL
FOUNDATION
PARTNERS WITH THE EARTH

30° 45° 60° 75° 90° 105° 120° 135° 150° 165° 180° 90°

75°

Arctic Circle

60°

SWEDEN
FINLAND
Oslo
Stockholm

SOVIET   UNION

45°

Moscow

POLAND
Berlin
MANY
CZECH.
AUS.
HUNG. ROM.
YUGOSLAVIA BUL.
ITALY
Rome
GREECE Istanbul
Athens TURKEY

MONGOLIA

International Date Line

Beijing
NORTH
KOREA
SOUTH

JAPAN
Tokyo

30°

CHINA

SYRIA
TUNISIA
Baghdad
ISRAEL IRAQ
Cairo
JORDAN
LIBYA
EGYPT

IRAN AFGHANISTAN

PAKISTAN Delhi NEPAL

Shanghai

Tropic of Cancer

TAIWAN

SAUDI
ARABIA

Calcutta MYANMAR
(BURMA)

HONG
KONG

15°

OMAN

INDIA

Bombay

LAOS

NIGER CHAD

YEMEN

THAILAND VIETNAM

Manila

SUDAN

CAM-
BODIA

PHILIPPINES

GERIA

SRI LANKA

CEN.
AFR. REP.
ETHIOPIA

SOMALIA

MALAYSIA

CAMEROON
UGANDA
Singapore

Equator 0°

GABON
CONGO KENYA
ZAIRE

PAPUA
NEW GUINEA

Jakarta INDONESIA

TANZANIA

15°

ANGOLA ZAMBIA

MADAGASCAR

ZIMBABWE

MOZAMBIQUE

Tropic of Capricorn

AUSTRALIA

BOTSWANA

NAMIBIA
Johannesburg

30°

SOUTH
AFRICA

Sydney

Cape Town

Auckland

Melbourne NEW
ZEALAND

45°

60°

Antarctic Circle

75°

TARCTICA

©1991 Rand McNally & Co. 90°

30° 45° 60° 75° 90° 105° 120° 135° 150° 165° 180° 90°

Kilometers 0 1000 2000 3000 Km.
Statute Miles 0 1000 2000 3000 Mi.

Rand McNally
Children's Atlas
of the
Environment

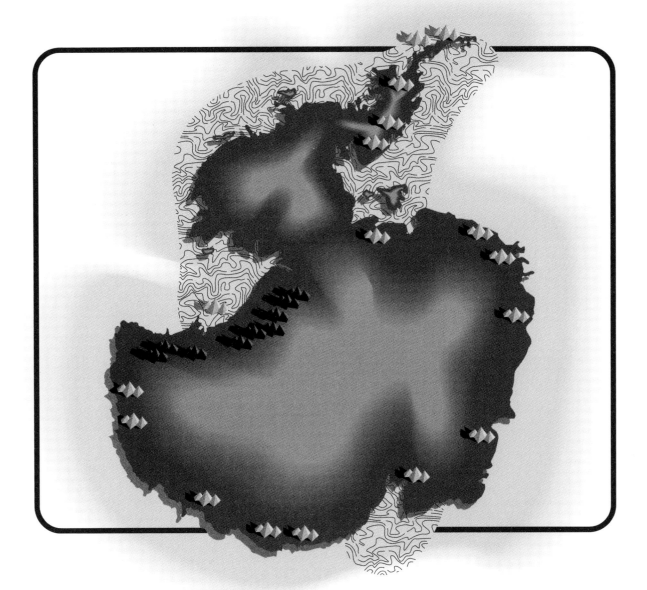

Rand McNally

Chicago • New York • San Francisco

Rand McNally Children's Atlas of the Environment

General manager: Russell L. Voisin
Managing editor: Jon M. Leverenz
Editor: Elizabeth G. Fagan
Writer: Jerry Sullivan
Designer: Corasue Nicholas
Computer graphics: Precision Graphics
Production editor: Laura C. Schmidt
Production manager: Patricia Martin

Rand McNally Children's Atlas of the Environment
Copyright © 1991 by Rand McNally & Company

All rights reserved. No part of this publication may be
reproduced, stored in a retrieval system, or transmitted,
in any form or by any means—electronic, mechanical,
photocopying, recording, or otherwise—without the
prior written permission of Rand McNally & Company.
Published and printed in the United States of America.

Photograph credits
Pages 8-9 Koalas: John Cancalosi/Tom Stack & Associates.Children: John Isaac/UNICEF. Lily & dragonfly: John Gerlach/Tom Stack & Associates. 10-11 Brown
bear: John Shaw/Tom Stack & Associates. 12-13 Mount St. Helens: AP/Wide World Photos. 14-15 England: David M. Dennis/Tom Stack & Associates. Polar bear:
Mark Newman/Tom Stack & Associates. 16-17 Hurricane Hugo: NOAA/NESDIS/NCDC/SDSD. 18-19 Oregon forest: Milton Rand/Tom Stack & Associates.
Prairie: Brian Parker/Tom Stack & Associates. 20-21 Subdivision: Gary Milburn/Tom Stack & Associates. 22-23 Nepalese woman: CARE photo by Rudolph von
Bernuth. Gary, Indiana: AP/Wide World Photos. 24-25 North Dakota: John Running. 26-27 Wind generators: Kevin Shafer/Tom Stack & Associates. 28-29
Treatment plant: Byron Augustin/Tom Stack & Associates. 30-31 Cleanup: AP/Wide World Photos. 32-33 Pines: Diana L. Stratton/Tom Stack & Associates. 34-35
Leopard: Jeff Foott/Tom Stack & Associates. 36-37 Family planning: CARE photo by Rudolph von Bernuth. 38-39 Norway: Spencer Swanger/Tom Stack &
Associates. Bulgaria: AP/Wide World Photos. 40-41 Black forest: Spencer Swanger/Tom Stack & Associates. Protesters: Chris Niedenthal/Time Magazine. 42-43
Turtle: Gary Milburn/Tom Stack & Associates. Nice, France: David C. London/Tom Stack & Associates. 44-45 Siberia: Boyd Norton. Tokyo: Sheryl S.
McNee/Tom Stack & Associates. 46-47 Aral Sea: David Turnley/Black Star. Lake Baikal: Boyd Norton. 48-49 Rain forest: Boyd Norton. Nepal: CARE photo by
Rudolph von Bernuth. 50-51 Clear cut: Don Rutledge/Tom Stack & Associates. Reforestation: CARE photo by Jon Burbank. 52-53 Zebra & wildebeest: Jeff
Foott/Tom Stack & Associates. Zimbabwe: Rod Allin/Tom Stack & Associates. 54-55 Senegal: Clyde McNair/AID. Niger: CARE photo by Cynthia Citron. 56-57
Outback: Greg Vaughn/Tom Stack & Associates. Sydney beach: Greg Vaughn/Tom Stack & Associates. 58-59 Kiwi: Buff Corsi/Tom Stack & Associates. Tuatara:
John Cancalosi/Tom Stack & Associates. 60-61 Mount Moran: Gerald & Buff Corsi/Tom Stack & Associates. Fields: Shattil/Rozinski/Tom Stack & Associates. 62-
63 Leakage: Gary Milburn/Tom Stack & Associates. Cleanup: Gary Milburn/Tom Stack & Associates. 64-65 Freeway: Jack Swenson/Tom Stack & Associates.
School: Stewart M. Green/Tom Stack & Associates. 66-67 Andes: Gary Milburn/Tom Stack & Associates. Lake Titicaca: Gary Milburn/Tom Stack & Associates.
68-69 Colombia: Clyde McNair/AID. Seedlings: Chip & Jill Isenhart/Tom Stack & Associates. 70-71 Penguins: Anna E. Zuckerman/Tom Stack & Associates.
Station: Dave Watts/Tom Stack & Associates. 72-73 Trash: Jack Stein Grove/Tom Stack & Associates. Lapps: Warren & Genny Garst/Tom Stack & Associates.

Library of Congress Cataloging-in-Publication Data

Rand McNally and Company.
    Children's atlas of the environment.
        p.   cm.
    Includes indexes and glossary.
    Summary: Maps and text portray the world's ecosystems,
environmental concerns, and positive suggestions of what can be done
to help the planet.
    ISBN 0–528–83438–X
    1. Man—Influence on nature—Maps. 2. Human ecology—Maps.
[1. Man—Influence on nature—Maps. 2. Human ecology—Maps.
3. Environmental protection—Maps.]   I. Rand McNally and Company.
II. Title.
G1046.G3R23 1991 <G&M>
304.2'0223—dc20   91-9395
                                                      CIP
                                                   MAP AC

Printed on recycled paper.

Contents

How the Earth Supports Living Things

The air on the planet Venus is almost hot enough to melt lead. Mars is so cold that its surface is frozen. Only on the earth, among the nine planets in our solar system, do soft breezes blow and gentle rains fall.

Nowhere else have we found the miracle of life.

All of the earth's wonderful creatures live on the narrow, outermost region of our planet. The creatures crawling across the bottom of the deepest ocean are just a few miles below the highest-flying birds. We call this narrow home of life the *biosphere*. Above the sphere of life, the air is too thin and cold for living things. A few miles below the earth's surface, solid rock melts.

Plants and animals live in communities called *biomes*. Trees and squirrels are parts of forest biomes. Sharks and seaweed are parts

Above: Koalas such as these live only in eucalyptus groves in Australia. Adults eat nothing but eucalyptus leaves. Humans have made changes in the koala's biome, and it has become a rare species.

Right: We humans are only one among the many millions of different kinds of living things that share our wonderful earth.

Insects and flowering plants are important parts of all living communities on land. This lily could not produce seeds without insects to pollinate it. The dragonfly is a hunter that feeds on smaller insects.

of ocean biomes. Squirrels depend on trees for places to nest and for seeds to eat. Seaweed is food for the small fish that sharks eat.

The forces that support life work in ways that we can understand. They form patterns. They combine together into systems. The systems act together to keep the earth a balanced home for life. In the next few pages, we will show you the systems that make our lives possible, the systems that keep the biosphere working. This section is called "The Earth as a Balanced System."

The second section of this atlas is called "Upsetting the Balance." It shows some of the things that happen when human beings upset the systems that make the biosphere work. And it shows some of the ways we can learn to live and work without upsetting the balance.

The third section is about the regions of the earth. In each region we first look at the environments of the region. Then we take a closer look at one or two environmental problems that are especially serious in that part of the world. We look at solutions to these problems as well. This section is called "Restoring Balance in the Earth's Regions."

All over the world, people are realizing that we must learn to live in harmony with natural systems. Our search for that harmony is among the forces that will sustain the biosphere in the future.

Life clings to the surface of the earth. Among all the planets and moons of our solar system, this is the only place where air, water, light, and warmth combine to make a home for living things.

The Life-Giving Energy of the Sun

Energy from the sun makes the biosphere work. This energy provides us with light, warmth, food, and even water. If you leave a glass of water in the sun for a few days, the water will disappear. The sun's energy has turned the liquid water into a gas like the air, and the gas has risen into the atmosphere.

Every day the sun pulls water from the oceans, from lakes and rivers, from the leaves of plants, and from the soil itself. The gas, called *water vapor*, rises into the sky. High in the air, it cools and becomes a liquid again. The liquid water forms clouds. From the clouds fall the rain and snow that make life on land possible.

Green plants have the wonderful ability to turn sunlight into food. The pigment *chlorophyll* that makes leaves green also captures the sun's energy. Green leaves put together water and the gas called carbon dioxide from the air and make *glucose*, a kind of sugar. This is the food that gives the plant the energy to grow. And this energy also feeds the grasshoppers, the cows, and the zebras that eat the plants. And it feeds the meadowlark that eats the grasshopper, the lion that eats the zebra, and the person who drinks the milk of the cow.

Tiny green water plants called *algae* capture the sun's energy. Small fish eat the algae. Large fish, such as salmon, eat smaller fish. Animals like the Alaskan brown bear eat the salmon and in this way get their share of the sun's energy.

The constant flow of energy from the sun moves through the bodies of living things and sustains the life of earth's creatures.

The Earth's Changing Face

Antarctica is the coldest place on earth. It is covered by ice thousands of feet thick. But in the ancient rocks of this icy continent, scientists have found the remains of tropical forests now hardened into coal. In India and Madagascar, near the equator, scientists have found traces of ancient glaciers.

Ice in India and coal in Antarctica are among the thousands of discoveries that proved that the earth's outer layer—the crust—is actually broken into pieces. We call these pieces *plates*. There are six large plates and several smaller ones. The plates float on a layer of weaker rock below them.

The plates move. Their movements shape the continents and build our mountains. The Himalayas, the highest mountains on earth, rose when the Indo-Australian Plate collided with the Eurasian Plate. In the middle of the Atlantic Ocean, lava rising from deep within the earth pushes the American and Eurasian plates apart. In California, the Pacific Plate slides past the American Plate. The movement shakes the earth. Near Japan, the Pacific Plate slides under the Eurasian Plate making more earthquakes and raising more volcanoes.

Subduction Zone

Ocean Ridge Zone

Subduction zones are places where two plates are moving toward each other. One plate slides under the other. Plates pull apart at ocean ridges. Lava wells up from below the plates and makes volcanoes. Movement of the plates produces earthquakes.

AMERICAN PLATE

CARIBBEAN PLATE

COCOS PLATE

PACIFIC PLATE

NAZCA PLATE

Movements of the plates that make the earth's crust constantly remake the earth. South America and Africa were once joined together. As their plates move apart at the ocean ridge in the mid-Atlantic, the distance between them slowly grows.

Mount St. Helens in the state of Washington is one of a row of volcanoes that stands over the unstable boundary between the American Plate and the Pacific Plate. The top of the mountain blew off in a huge eruption in 1980.

EURASIAN PLATE

PACIFIC PLATE

PHILIPPINE PLATE

AFRICAN PLATE

INDO-AUSTRALIAN PLATE

ANTARCTIC PLATE

The Ways of Water

Watch water drain from a sink or bathtub. It doesn't go straight down the drain. It swirls. In the Northern Hemisphere, it swirls clockwise. In the Southern Hemisphere, it swirls counterclockwise. The daily rotation of the earth on its axis creates a force called the *Coriolis effect*. Coriolis force creates the swirls in your bathtub.

Now look on the map of the world's oceans. Notice the patterns of the currents. Currents are like rivers in the ocean. They flow only in water near the surface. They are driven by the winds and bent by Coriolis force into huge circles called *gyres*. The gyres turn clockwise in the Northern Hemisphere and counterclockwise in the Southern Hemisphere.

Water moves in the ocean depths as well. Cold water from the poles flows toward the equator, sliding under the lighter, warmer waters of the tropics. Off the coast of Peru, winds blow the warmer waters away and cold waters flowing north from Antarctica rise to the surface. These waters are rich in minerals and oxygen. They can support large numbers of living things. One-seventh of the world's catch of fish comes from this one small area.

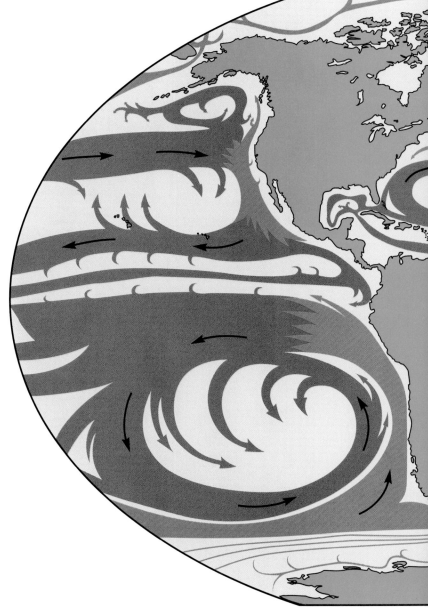

An ocean current called the Gulf Stream carries warm water from the Gulf of Mexico to the northern coasts of Europe. English farmland *(left)* is warmed by the Gulf Stream. It is much colder at the same latitude in Canada, where no Gulf Stream flows. So cold, in fact, that these parts are within the range of polar bears *(far left)*.

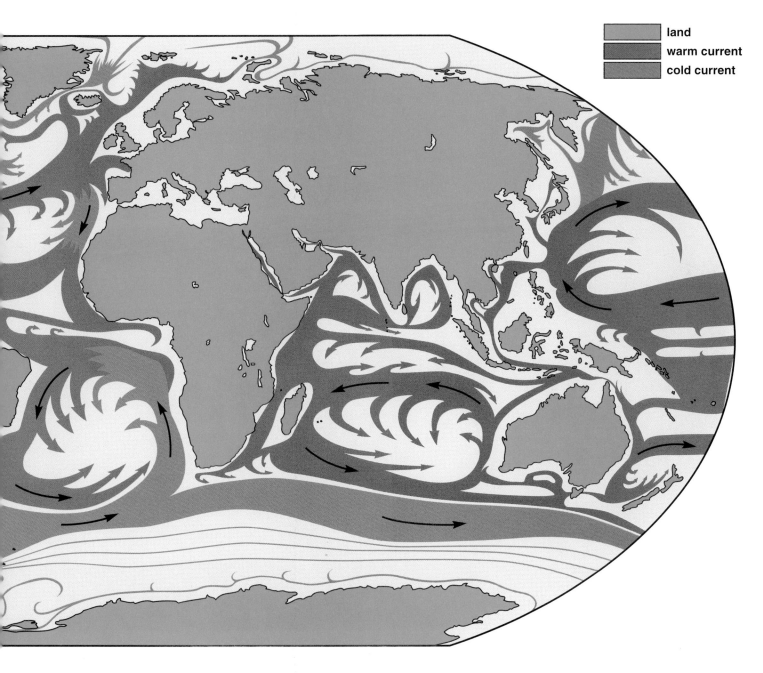

land

warm current

cold current

The Ways of Air

The air is an ocean too. Its currents are called winds. The daily changes in our ocean of air are called *weather*. It is hard to see patterns in the weather. It changes so often. But if we keep track of the weather through many years, we begin to see patterns in wind direction, rainfall, and temperature. We call these regular patterns *climate*.

There is a worldwide pattern in wind direction. Near the equator, the winds usually blow from the east. Between the tropics and the Arctic and Antarctic circles, they usually blow from the west. Winds are air moving across the face of the earth. But air also moves up and down.

At the equator, air rises. It cools as it rises.

Far right: The effect of Coriolis force on winds is clearly shown in this picture of a hurricane in the Atlantic Ocean off the southeastern coast of the United States. The winds are blowing toward the center of the hurricane.

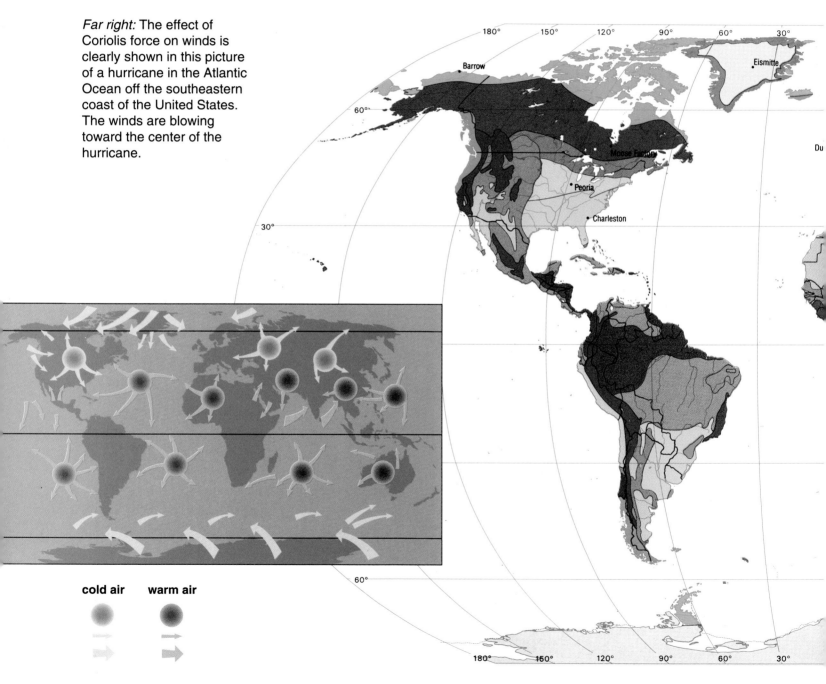

cold air   warm air

Its water vapor turns into a liquid and falls as rain. Climate near the equator is usually very wet. Near the Tropics of Cancer and Capricorn, the air is sinking. As it sinks, it grows warmer. The water remains vapor. Rainfall is scarce. Most of the world's deserts are near the tropics. North and south of the tropics, rising air produces more rainfall.

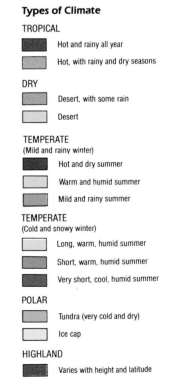

Copyright © 1991 by Rand McNally & Co.

Types of Climate

TROPICAL

- Hot and rainy all year
- Hot, with rainy and dry seasons

DRY

- Desert, with some rain
- Desert

TEMPERATE
(Mild and rainy winter)

- Hot and dry summer
- Warm and humid summer
- Mild and rainy summer

TEMPERATE
(Cold and snowy winter)

- Long, warm, humid summer
- Short, warm, humid summer
- Very short, cool, humid summer

POLAR

- Tundra (very cold and dry)
- Ice cap

HIGHLAND

- Varies with height and latitude

The World's Vegetation

Look at the map of the world's vegetation on this page. Now turn back one page, and look at the map of the world's climates. The two maps are not exactly the same, but they are very similar. Notice that the world's rain forests grow in the warm, wet climates along the equator. Notice that the low, creeping plants of the tundra grow in polar climates.

These similarities are not accidental. Plants can grow only where the climate suits them. We say they are *adapted* to a climate. In the very cold, dry lands at the edge of the Arctic, small plants that hug the ground and stay out of the wind are the only ones that can survive. Grasses grow in dry places where there is not enough water for trees. Where there is more rainfall, trees cast so much shade that the sun-loving grasses cannot grow.

Plants grow in communities. Tundra communities may have fewer than one hundred kinds of plants. Rain forest communities have thousands. The plants in communities depend on each other. Many forest wildflowers can grow only in the shade of tall trees. Some can grow only in the shade of certains kinds of trees. If those trees are taken from the forest, the flowers will disappear, too.

In the cool, wet climate along the Pacific Coast in the northern United States and southern Canada grow rich evergreen forests like this one in Oregon.

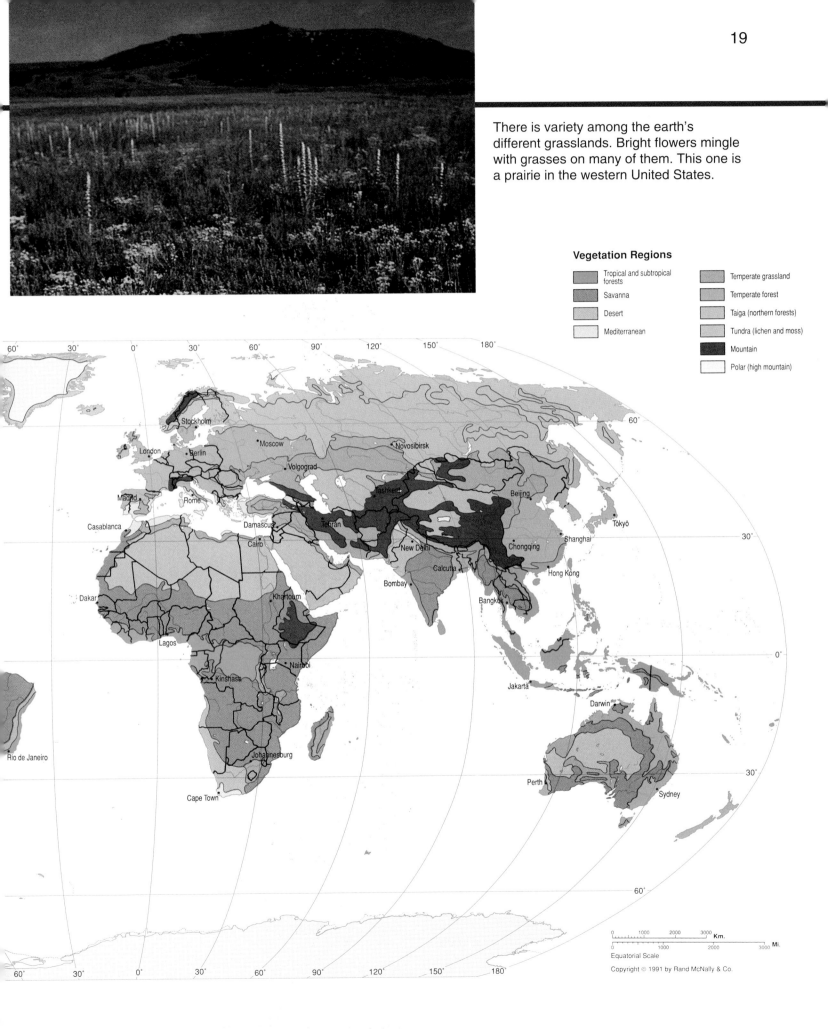

There is variety among the earth's different grasslands. Bright flowers mingle with grasses on many of them. This one is a prairie in the western United States.

Vegetation Regions

- Tropical and subtropical forests
- Savanna
- Desert
- Mediterranean
- Temperate grassland
- Temperate forest
- Taiga (northern forests)
- Tundra (lichen and moss)
- Mountain
- Polar (high mountain)

Stockholm
London
Berlin
Moscow
Novosibirsk
Volgograd
Madrid
Rome
Tashkent
Beijing
Casablanca
Damascus
Tehran
Tōkyō
Cairo
Shanghai
New Delhi
Chongqing
Calcutta
Hong Kong
Bombay
Dakar
Khartoum
Bangkok
Lagos
Nairobi
Kinshasa
Jakarta
Darwin
Rio de Janeiro
Johannesburg
Perth
Sydney
Cape Town

0   1000   2000   3000 Km.
0   1000   2000   3000 Mi.
Equatorial Scale

Copyright © 1991 by Rand McNally & Co.

The World's Population

Humans began to spread across the earth from Africa, the birthplace of humanity, about two million years ago. Humans moved north into Asia and Europe, then east toward the Pacific. During the Ice Age, when there was a land connection between Siberia and Alaska, they crossed into the Americas.

Now humans live all over the world. For the first time in the history of the earth, one kind of animal, a single species, controls the whole planet. Other animals and plants can live only where conditions are right for them: polar bears and pine trees could not live in the desert; camels and cacti could not survive deep snow and icy winds.

Humans can live in so many different kinds of places because we have learned to invent the things we need. We have made clothes to keep us warm. We have invented tools to help us hunt for food. We can live by the sea because we have invented boats, nets, and hooks to help catch fish. We can bring water to the desert from wells and pipelines.

Our inventions have given us so much power that we could even put an end to life on earth. Now we must all work to discover ways to live in the world without destroying it.

Growing populations have moved into suburban developments like this one in the United States. The developments replace natural areas and land that was used for farming.

Population Density
Per square mile

Uninhabited	60-125 inhabitants
Under 2 inhabitants	125-250 inhabitants
2-25 inhabitants	Over 250 inhabitants
25-60 inhabitants	

- Metropolitan areas over 2,000,000 population
- Metropolitan areas 1,000,000 to 2,000,000 population

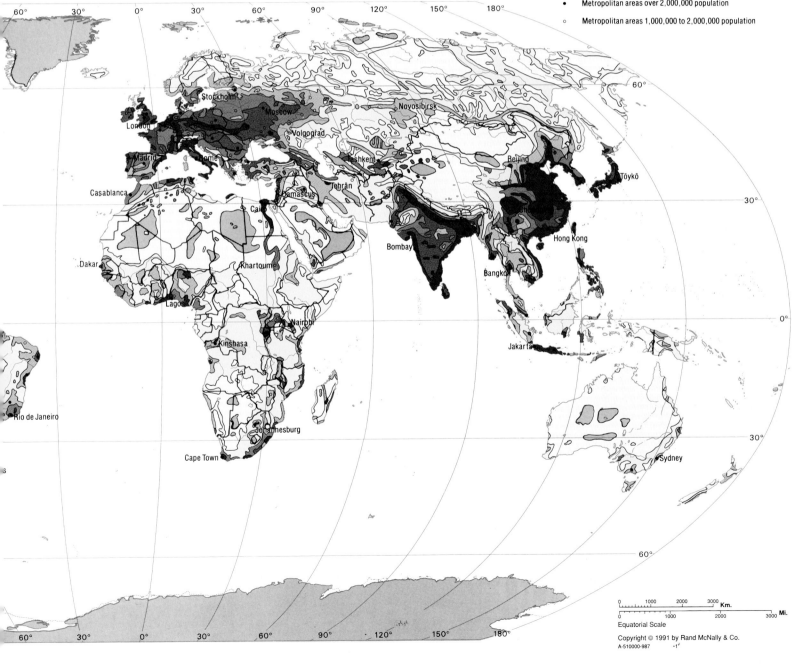

0   1000   2000   3000 Km.
0   1000   2000   3000 Mi.
Equatorial Scale

Copyright © 1991 by Rand McNally & Co.
A-510000-987   -1'

How People Use the Land

A griculture is one of the most important inventions in human history. Before they learned how to grow crops and keep animals, all people were wanderers. They moved from place to place to follow the animals they hunted or to gather wild plants.

Agriculture allowed humans to settle down. They built towns and cities. As farmers got better at growing food, more people were free to do other things. They could spend their days making pottery or learning to work with metal.

As people began to explore new ways of doing things, more inventions followed. Machinery began to replace human labor. Huge factories began to replace small family workshops.

Human populations grew. Farmers cleared forests and plowed prairies in the search for more land to feed all the people. Huge cities grew. Some spread so far they met other cities and formed large urban areas. In the eastern United States, a strip of land with New York City at its center forms an almost continuous city three hundred miles long!

As the map shows, we have changed the world in big ways. Croplands and grazing lands have replaced forests and grasslands in many areas. We have changed the earth so much, it is showing signs of stress. The next section tells of these stresses—the ways in which humans are upsetting the balance.

Above, left: Agriculture was the invention that made civilization possible. It also uses more land than any other human activity.

Above, right: Industry and cities make very intensive use of the land. In Gary, Indiana, thousands work in the steel mill in the background. Thousands more live and work in the buildings in the foreground.

Environments

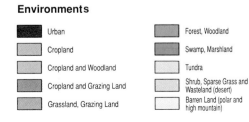

Urban	Forest, Woodland
Cropland	Swamp, Marshland
Cropland and Woodland	Tundra
Cropland and Grazing Land	Shrub, Sparse Grass and Wasteland (desert)
Grassland, Grazing Land	Barren Land (polar and high mountain)

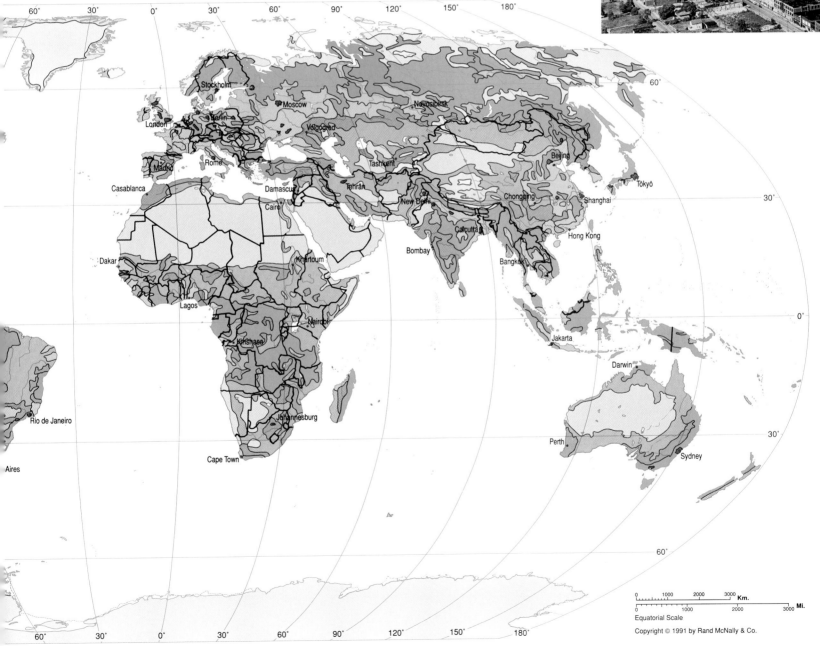

Stockholm
Moscow
London
Berlin
Novosibirsk
Madrid
Rome
Volgograd
Casablanca
Damascus
Tashkent
Beijing
Cairo
Tehrān
Tōkyō
New Delhi
Chongqing
Shanghai
Dakar
Khartoum
Calcutta
Hong Kong
Bombay
Lagos
Bangkok
Nairobi
Kinshasa
Jakarta
Rio de Janeiro
Darwin
Johannesburg
Perth
Cape Town
Sydney
Aires

Equatorial Scale

Copyright © 1991 by Rand McNally & Co.

Destroying the Soil

In this section, we will look at global environmental problems. These problems are caused by human actions that interfere with the natural balance on which all living things depend. When we break these natural patterns, we can be sure that problems will arise.

Nature makes the soil that grows the crops that feed us. When we plow the land to plant crops, we leave the ground bare. Wind and water can carry away the bare soil. This process is called *erosion*. Although it is a natural process, it happens much faster on plowed land than on land covered with grass or trees. The wind and water can carry away minerals that feed plants. Erosion robs the soil of its ability to grow plants, or *fertility*.

Plants need minerals from the soil to help them grow. Farmers use *fertilizers* to replace the lost minerals. They also use *pesticides* to kill weeds and harmful insects. Some kinds of fertilizers and pesticides pollute wells, lakes, and rivers and kill animals.

Farmers are looking for better ways. Some are trying *organic farming*. They are farming without chemicals. They use animal manure or dead plants for fertilizers. They use natural methods to control pests. Farmers who *irrigate* their crops are finding ways to grow food with much less water. Irrigation water sometimes puts salt into the soil. Crops cannot grow in salty soils. Less water means less salt.

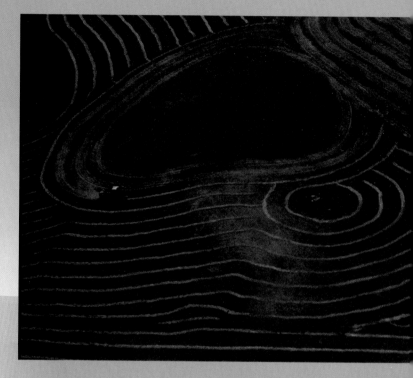

This drawing shows some ways in which we are destroying the soil and some of the harmful effects of soil destruction. Spray-type irrigation systems lose large amounts of water through evaporation. Water running off fields may carry pesticides and excess fertilizers into lakes and streams.

How Can We Help?

- By irrigating crops in ways that apply water directly to plants and do not lose large amounts of water to evaporation.

- By using as few pesticides as possible. And by continuing to find ways to control insects and other pests without using chemical pesticides.

- By using contour plowing and other farming methods that control soil erosion.

Contour plowing means plowing furrows that follow the shape of the land. The furrows run across slopes, not up and down them. Contour plowing stops rainwater from rushing down slopes. This prevents erosion and helps us stop destroying the soil.

Spraying pesticides from airplanes to control insects or plant diseases spreads these chemicals through the whole environment. They can harm other animals and humans as well.

By plowing straight up and down the hillside, this farmer is increasing the amount of soil he loses to erosion. Soil carried away by water can turn clear streams muddy.

Polluting the Air

Every moment, all of us are affecting the atmosphere. Plants take the gas carbon dioxide (CO_2) from the air and return oxygen. Animals breathe in oxygen and breathe out CO_2. The air protects us. It blocks dangerous x-rays, gamma rays, and ultraviolet rays from the sun.

Now we have upset the balance. By burning coal and oil, we release carbon that was locked up underground millions of years ago. The amount of CO_2 in the air is growing. Carbon dioxide holds the sun's heat in the atmosphere just as the glass roof of a greenhouse holds heat in the greenhouse. Many scientists believe that more CO_2 will create a *greenhouse effect*. The earth will get warmer, causing harmful changes in our climate.

A group of gases called *chlorofluorocarbons* are contributing to the greenhouse effect. They are also destroying the *ozone layer*, a part of the atmosphere that protects us from the sun's ultraviolet radiation. These gases, often called *CFCs*, are used in refrigerators, air conditioners, and some aerosol spray cans. When they escape they rise high into the air. There they meet *ozone*, a kind of oxygen that stops ultraviolet rays. They break up the ozone and let ultraviolet rays through to the earth.

These wind generators at Altamont Pass in California produce electricity without releasing carbon dioxide. Using wind and solar power instead of coal and oil helps reduce the greenhouse effect and helps us stop polluting the air.

This drawing shows ways in which we are polluting the air and some of the harmful effects of air pollution. Burning tropical forests to clear the land releases large amounts of CO_2 into the air.

Coal and oil burned to heat buildings and as fuel for industry add still more carbon dioxide to the atmosphere.

Ozone, an oxygen molecule made of three oxygen atoms, blocks ultraviolet rays high above the earth.

Ultraviolet rays reaching the earth's surface damage plants and can cause skin cancer in humans.

How Can We Help?

- By using energy efficiently to get the most out of every barrel of oil or ton of coal.

- By using solar or wind power instead of burning fuels.

- By carrying out international agreements to end the use of chlorofluorocarbons by the year 2000.

Exhaust fumes from cars and trucks are helping increase CO_2 in the air by almost 2 percent a year.

Dirtying the Fresh Water

Fresh water all began as rain or snow. Much of it is frozen into the ice caps of Greenland and Antarctica. Some of the unfrozen fresh water is in lakes and rivers, but most is under the ground. It is held in tiny pores in rock. It is found by digging wells. About half the people in the United States use this *ground water* for drinking.

Humanity misuses this precious fresh water in two ways. It is wasted through careless use and polluted by dumping wastes into it. People build large cities in deserts and grow crops in dry valleys. In the American West, so much water is taken out of the Colorado River that there is none left to flow into the sea. In the world's dry places, people must learn to avoid waste, to make every gallon count.

People pollute water by dumping sewage and industrial wastes into it or by letting pesticides from farmland run into it. Even ground water is polluted by poisons sinking into the earth. Humanity must learn that nothing just "goes away." People need to treat sewage so it does not pollute the water. They need to keep industrial wastes completely out of the water.

This drawing shows ways in which we are dirtying and wasting our fresh water. Mining often releases toxic substances such as sulfuric acid, lead, and arsenic into local waters.

Wastewater treatment plants, like this one in Austin, Texas, clean water from sewers so it can be returned to lakes and rivers without polluting them. This is a way we can stop dirtying our fresh water.

Three-fourths of the water humans use is for irrigation. Most of this is lost to evaporation. Only one-third of irrigation water reaches crops.

Runoff from farms carries sediments, pesticides, and excess fertilizers.

Humans take so much water from some rivers that little reaches the sea. Marshlands near the river mouth may dry up.

How Can We Help?

- By getting the most out of every drop of water we use in our households, farms, and businesses.

- By treating wastewater from mines, factories, and households to remove pollutants. The water we pour into the river should be as pure as the water we take from it.

- By preserving wetlands. Swamps and marshes are natural ways to purify water.

Dams give us electricity and reliable sources of water, but in dry regions, they lose much water to evaporation.

Twenty percent of the water we use goes to industry. Often wastewater is returned to rivers in a very polluted state.

Only about 5 percent of our water is for household use. But untreated sewage is a big source of pollution.

Fouling the Salt Water

The oceans cover 70 percent of the earth. They are so big, it is hard to imagine people could do anything to harm them. But we have.

Most of the plants and animals in the ocean live near the shore. Many fish and shellfish spend the early parts of their lives right at the shore in marshes or thickets of *mangrove* trees. *Coral reefs* in shallow waters are homes for thousands of different animals. People can harm the oceans just because so much of these animals' lives are spent near the shores where human mistakes can affect them.

People dump garbage and sewage and spill oil into the oceans. Rivers carry industrial wastes to the sea. The ocean is also harmed when marshes and mangrove thickets are destroyed to make room for buildings on the shore. The animals who

How Can We Help?

- By protecting mangroves, salt marshes, coral reefs, and other sensitive areas on and near the ocean's shores.

- By strengthening existing international agreements to limit whaling and expanding them to include important species of fish.

- By supporting and expanding international agreements that forbid waste dumping in the oceans.

Drilling platforms that tap undersea oil deposits are sometimes the sources of serious spills.

Only a few thousand humpbacked whales and sperm whales are left in the oceans. They are victims of the whaling industry.

This drawing shows ways in which we are fouling and harming the oceans. Eroded soil, brought to the ocean in rivers, disturbs the fragile life of the world's coral reefs.

need these thickets and marshes are left without a home. Some of the larger whales have been so heavily hunted they are almost extinct. Heavy fishing has lowered the numbers of some kinds of fish.

Recently, the world's industrial countries agreed to gradually stop dumping wastes in the oceans. Although many countries have agreed to stop whaling, stronger agreements on whales are needed, as are similar agreements for fish.

Workers scrub the beaches of Prince William Sound near Valdez, Alaska. The shores were coated with oil from the largest spill in U.S. history. This was a small step we took to help us stop fouling the salt water.

One-third of the oil in the ocean comes from tankers. More is dumped deliberately, when tanks are cleaned, than accidentally.

Long drift nets pulled behind ships catch everything in their path. Dolphins, turtles, and seabirds are caught as well as large numbers of fish.

The loss of mangrove swamps and beaches harms sea turtles, manatees, and many other ocean animals.

Stripping Away Plant Life

Plants and animals live in communities. Communities need space. They need enough room to provide a *habitat* or home to populations of all their species. If there is only one pair of robins in a woodland, a single accident can destroy the species. If there is a population of robins, the species can survive even though individuals die.

Populations of some small plants and animals can survive in a community little bigger than a football field. Larger plants and animals, and many smaller ones as well, need much more space. As we humans have spread around the world, we have cut forests and plowed prairies. Our farms and cities have taken much of the space that was once a home for natural communities.

Many of the rare and endangered species in the world are in danger simply because they have no place to live. Their habitats have been turned into cities and farms. Many countries have national parks and other preserves that give communities a home. We need to protect these and expand them. We need to remember that we share the earth with millions of other creatures. They have a right to live, too.

After a natural fire burned this pine woods in Grand Teton National Park, Wyoming, a new crop of seedlings began to grow. Letting nature heal itself is one way we can stop stripping away plant life.

This drawing shows ways in which we are stripping away plant life. Draining and filling marshes, swamps, and other wetlands have eliminated plants in many places around the world.

How Can We Help?

- By setting aside lands as parks and preserves where natural communities can be protected. And by knowing how valuable our wetlands are to us and to other living things and protecting all we have left.

- By cutting wood in ways that disturb forests as little as possible.

- By making the best use we can of land in our cities and on our farms.

Logging methods called *clearcutting* take every tree from the forest. The bare soil erodes easily, and plants and animals that need old forests are left without homes.

Spreading cities have taken both farmland and natural land. Farming methods that use every bit of land for growing crops also take habitat away from wild plants and animals.

Threatening Animal Life

Humans have been hunters for as long as they have been human. People hunted for food. They hunted for skins to turn into clothing. They hunted for bear teeth and eagle feathers for decoration.

Once, human weapons were spears and arrows. Now weapons are automatic rifles and harpoons fired from cannons. Humans are chasing animals whose populations are already low because much of their living space has been taken by people. Once, people killed animals for food or clothing. Now hunting is a big business. African rhino horns are sold in China. Elephant ivory and leopard skins from Africa are sold all over the world. Animal skins are made into expensive fur coats.

Pollution also kills animals. The bald eagle was almost destroyed by the pesticide DDT. Seals in the Baltic Sea are dying from diseases caused by pollution.

All the world must work together to protect these persecuted animals. African nations may want help in stopping illegal hunting. All nations need to stop the buying and selling of horns, ivory, and skins taken from these animals. And all nations must stop the pollution that kills both animals and humans.

Hyacinth Macaw

Sperm Whale

Protecting wild animals makes economic sense to nations that attract tourists interested in wildlife. Setting aside preserves such as this one in Kenya helps us stop threatening animal life.

This drawing shows some of the many animals that are threatened. Sperm whales have long been targets of the whaling industry. South America's parrots and monkeys are threatened by the pet trade. So many have been caught and sold as pets that some species are in danger of becoming extinct in the wild. Elephants and rhinoceroses are slaughtered for their tusks and horns. Despite the protection of being classified as an endangered species, the snow leopard of the Himalayas is still hunted for its beautiful fur.

How Can We Help?

- By gaining the cooperation of all countries to control buying and selling of endangered animals. Most countries are part of the Convention on International Trade in Endangered Species (CITES), but this agreement must be made stronger.

- By encouraging effective systems of parks and preserves that give habitat to endangered species.

- By knowing that all the earth's animals have a right to live their lives, too.

Snow Leopard

Elephant

Golden Lion Tamarin

Rhinoceros

Crowding Human Life

In 1950, there were only 2.5 billion people in the world. Now there are 5.3 billion. Human population may reach 8.5 billion by the year 2025. Experts disagree about how serious a problem this very fast growth is. And they disagree about what should be done about it.

It could be said that growth is slowing down. Most industrial countries—Japan, Canada, the United States, and the nations of Europe—are hardly growing at all. In Asia, Africa, and Latin America, growth is somewhat slower than it was twenty years ago.

Industrial nations all went through a time of fast growth when their industry was developing. When they reached the point where most people could live in comfort, population growth slowed. Many experts believe that today's *developing nations* will go through a similar change. The best way to control population, they say, is to raise the standard of living.

Industrial nations are beginning to look for ways to produce goods without the pollution that is one of the harmful effects of overcrowding. Developing countries will also use such methods if they are to take care of their people. Educating children everywhere is expensive, but the cost is worthwhile because children will contribute to their country's development when they are grown. Perhaps children now in school will invent ways to help people live at peace with the earth.

How Can We Help?

- By supporting educational programs that help people learn how to control the growth of their families.

- By helping people get the food and medical care they need to raise healthy children.

United States

Mexico

Brazil

Chile

population increase per year

more than 3%

2%–3%

1%–2%

less than 1%

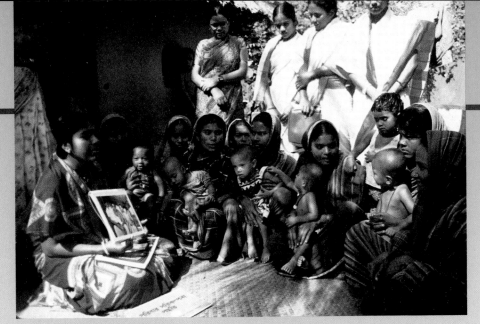

Women in a village in Bangladesh attend a class in child care. Raising healthy babies is an important part of family planning. And family planning helps us stop human life from getting too crowded.

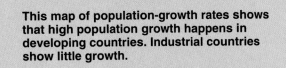

This map of population-growth rates shows that high population growth happens in developing countries. Industrial countries show little growth.

Europe: Environments

The Industrial Revolution began in Europe. It was here that the steam engine was first used to drive the machines in the first large factories. Industry is still the heart of the European economy, and industrial pollution is the most serious environmental problem.

Cities, industrial centers, and farms that have been cultivated for centuries cover almost all the land in western Europe. Even the forests are carefully planted and tended. Most Europeans live in towns. Only in Yugoslavia and Albania do most of the people live on farms. Land in a natural state still exists in the far north and in eastern Europe. In these areas, large native animals such as wild boars and wolves can still be found.

Throughout their long history, the nations of Europe have often been divided and in conflict with each other. But in recent years, the idea of a common European home has inspired the people of the continent. Winds do not stop at international borders and the same seas touch the shores of many lands. European nations are now working together on solutions to the environmental problems of their common home.

Above: Heavy industry and traditional farms often exist side-by-side in Europe. Here a Bulgarian shepherd tends his flock next to a huge industrial complex.

Right: This rugged landscape along the coast of Norway shows one of the few wilderness spots left on the European continent.

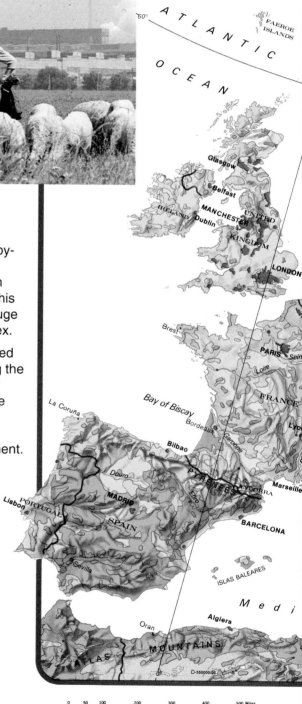

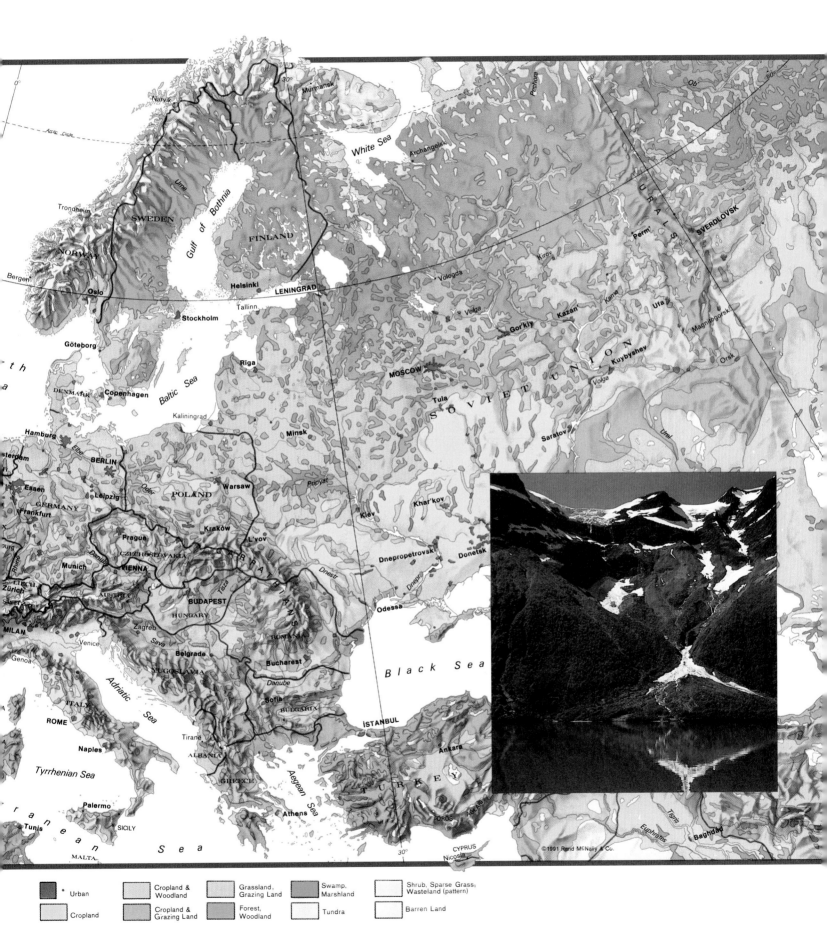

0°

30°

Arctic Circle

Narvik

Murmansk

White Sea

Archangelsk

Trondheim

SWEDEN

NORWAY

Bergen

Oslo

Göteborg

Helsinki

LENINGRAD

Tallinn

Stockholm

Rīga

DENMARK Copenhagen

Baltic Sea

Hamburg

Kaliningrad

Minsk

Essen

BERLIN

GERMANY

Frankfurt

Leipzig

POLAND

Warsaw

Odra

Prague

Kraków

L'vov

Munich

CZECHOSLOVAKIA

VIENNA

AUSTRIA

CARPATHIAN

BUDAPEST

HUNGARY

Zagreb

Sava

Tisza

ROMANIA

Bucharest

Belgrade

YUGOSLAVIA

Danube

Sofia

BULGARIA

Tirane

ALBANIA

GREECE

ROME

Naples

Tyrrhenian Sea

Palermo

SICILY

Tunis

MALTA

Mediterranean Sea

Athens

Aegean Sea

İSTANBUL

Ankara

TURKEY

Black Sea

Odessa

Dnestr

Dnepro

Dnepr

Kiev

Khar'kov

Dnepropetrovsk

Donetsk

Pripyat

Gulf of Bothnia

FINLAND

Ume

Vologda

Volga

Gor'kiy

Kazan

Kama

Perm'

URALS

SVERDLOVSK

Kirov

Ufa

Magnitogorsk

MOSCOW

Tula

Orsk

Kuybyshev

SOVIET UNION

Volga

Saratov

Ural

Pechora

Ob'

60°

60°

MILAN

Venice

Genoa

Adriatic Sea

ITALY

Zürich

LIECH

Danube

Rhine

30°

CYPRUS

Nicosia

TOROS

AĞRI

Tigris

Euphrates

Baghdad

©1991 Rand McNally & Co.

■ Urban	Cropland & Woodland	Grassland, Grazing Land	Swamp, Marshland	Shrub, Sparse Grass, Wasteland (pattern)	
Cropland	Cropland & Grazing Land	Forest, Woodland	Tundra	Barren Land	

Europe: Who Can Stop the Rain?

When coal or oil is burned, sulfur and nitrogen in the fuels combine with oxygen and escape into the air. Once in the air, they are changed into sulfuric acid and nitric acid. These acids fall to earth in rain and snow.

Acid rain has killed almost all the plants and animals in ten thousand lakes in Sweden. In western Germany, more than half the forests are damaged. In parts of Czechoslovakia and Romania, evergreen trees are dead or dying.

Dealing with acid rain is very hard in Europe because the continent has so many countries. Pollution that hurts one country may come from another country. Who should pay to correct the problem: the country that makes the pollution or the country harmed by it?

A United Nations agency has recommended as a first step that sulfur dioxide emissions be reduced by 30 percent and nitrogen oxide emissions frozen at 1980 levels. Twenty-one countries have agreed to this goal. After long discussions, twelve western European nations have agreed on a plan to reduce sulfur dioxide emissions by 60 percent and nitrogen oxide emissions by 30 percent.

Concerned citizens have inspired European governments to take major actions to improve the environment. Here, Europeans sign petitions in support of a clean environment.

Acid rain is killing trees such as these in Germany's Black Forest. In some woodlands, as many as half the trees have been damaged or killed.

How Can We Help?

- By bringing more countries into discussions on how to set even lower limits on emissions in the future.

- By continuing to look for cleaner ways to generate electricity and make industrial goods.

Naturally acid soils combine with winds that carry industrial pollution to make some parts of Europe subject to heavy damage from acid rain.

acidity of rain

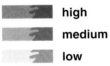

high

medium

low

Europe: A Fragile Sea

The Mediterranean is a very fragile sea. Water does not flow out of it. Water flows in at Gibraltar, the Suez Canal, and the Black Sea, but only evaporation takes water out. Pollutants dumped in the Mediterranean stay in it.

One hundred million people live on the shores of this sea. Eighteen countries share its coasts. In 1976, seventeen of these countries held a meeting in Barcelona, Spain, to work out ways to protect the Mediterranean. All eighteen coastal countries are now part of this group.

The countries have set aside fifteen reserves to protect endangered species such as the Mediterranean monk seal. And they have agreed to stop dumping such dangerous substances as lead, DDT, mercury, and cadmium into the water. Oil tankers can no longer wash out their holds at sea. Laboratories in many coastal nations are monitoring the state of the sea.

Much remains to be done. Many cities on the coast do not have modern sewage treatment plants. Much pollution from industry still flows into the sea. But the cooperative efforts of many nations are beginning to pay off. Meetings continue to plan more actions to help save the Mediterranean.

Above: Special agreements among Mediterranean countries are now providing protection for endangered sea animals such as the loggerhead turtle shown here.

Below: Crowded shoreline scenes like this one are common in this part of the world. Pollution from the large population that lives on the shores of the Mediterranean is one of the problems that the countries around the sea must work to control.

How Can We Help?

- By continuing the international action begun by the Barcelona Convention of 1976.

- By controlling industrial pollution and dumping of sewage into the sea. And by controlling dumping of oil by tankers.

- By increasing efforts to provide protection for birds, mammals, turtles, and other creatures that live in the Mediterranean.

This drawing shows the sources of major problems in the Mediterranean. Industrial pollution, sewage, oil spills, and overfishing all contribute to the dirtying of the water.

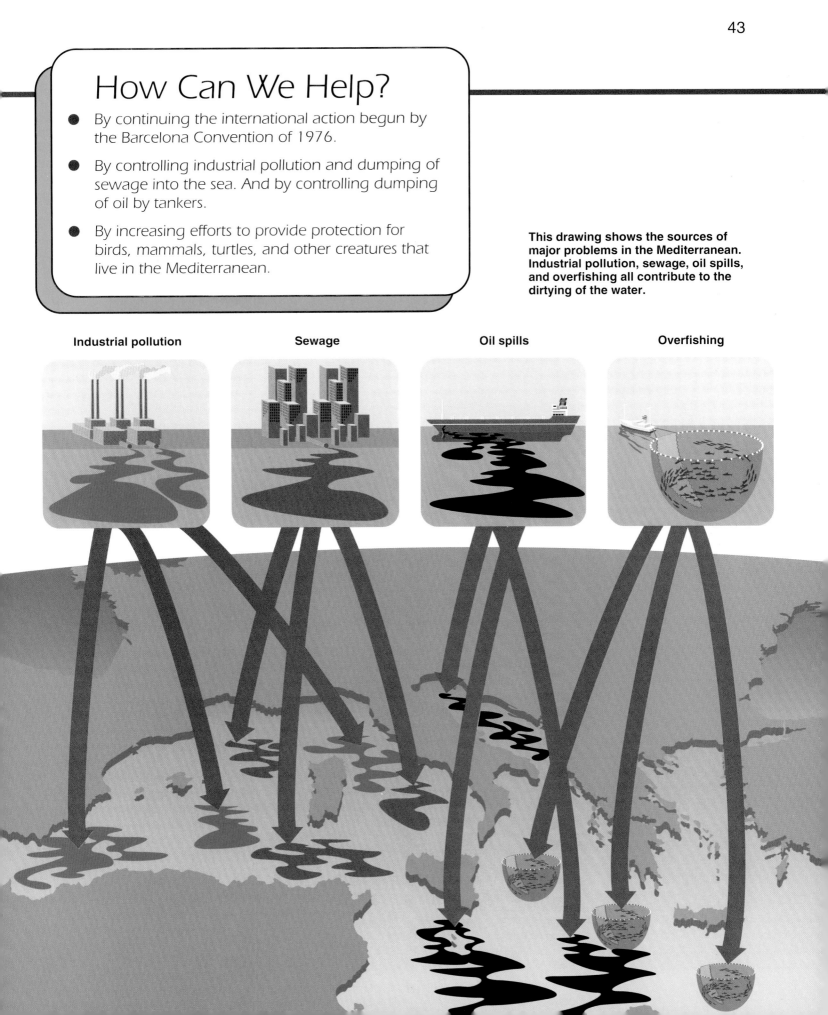

Industrial pollution   **Sewage**   **Oil spills**   **Overfishing**

Northern Asia: Environments

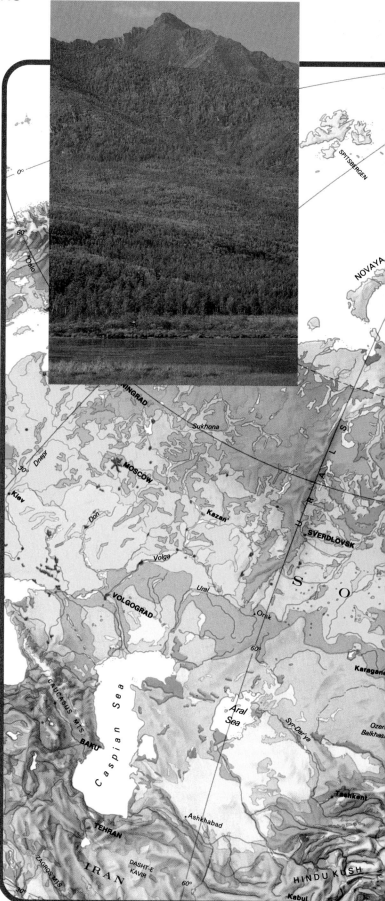

Across the vast reaches of northern Asia, many different life-styles can be found. In the east is Japan with its modern industries and crowded cities. In northern China, peasants plow the same soil that supported their ancestors two thousand years ago. On the plains of Mongolia, nomadic herders follow their animals in search of good pasture. In northern Siberia, hunting peoples still seek seals and reindeer just as their ancestors did.

In the far north is the treeless land of the *tundra*. Just south of that is a huge forest of spruce, fir, and other evergreen trees called the *taiga*. Few people live on the tundra or in the taiga. Wolves, brown bears, and even tigers still roam the wilderness.

In recent years, more people have been moving into these remote areas. The land is rich in minerals, and the forests can supply timber for homes and wood pulp for making paper. These industries have begun to change the face of northern Asia. Similar industries are growing in northern China and in Korea. Without careful planning, these new industries may bring with them the same pollution problems that have troubled Europe and North America.

Above, left: Rugged mountains and vast forests are typical of the wilderness of Siberia. Human settlements in this part of Northern Asia are few and widely scattered.

Above, right: Vast and sprawling Tokyo, Japan, is one of the world's largest cities. Northern Asia also contains the huge cities of Beijing, Shanghai, and Seoul.

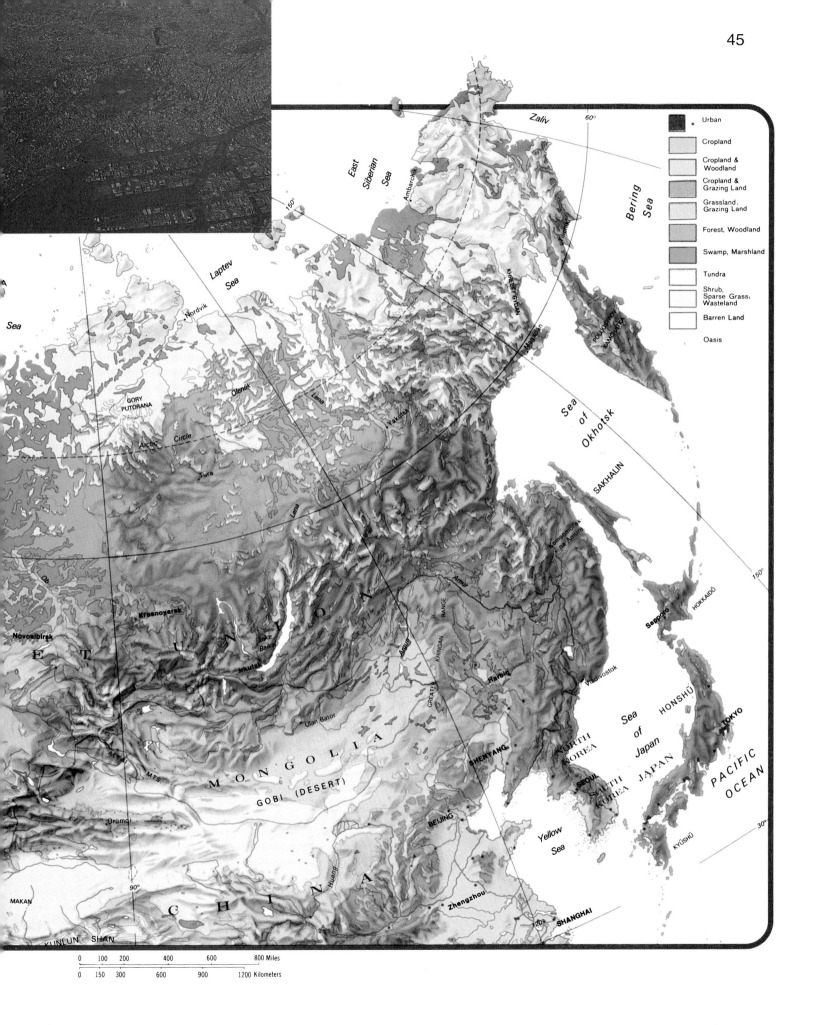

Urban
Cropland
Cropland &
Woodland
Cropland &
Grazing Land
Grassland,
Grazing Land
Forest, Woodland
Swamp, Marshland
Tundra
Shrub,
Sparse Grass;
Wasteland
Barren Land

Oasis

Zaliv   60°

East
Siberian
Sea

Bering
Sea

Laptev
Sea

Ambarchik

KHREBET GYDAN

POLUOSTROV
KAMCHATKA

Magadan

Nordvik

Sea

GORY
PUTORANA

Olenëk

Lena

Arctic   Circle

Yakutsk

Sea
of
Okhotsk

Jura

SAKHALIN

Lena

Komsomolsk
na-Amure

Ob

Amur

HOKKAIDŌ

150°

Krasnoyarsk

Sapporo

RANGE

Novosibirsk

ET   UN   ION

Lake
Baikal

Amur

GREATER KHINGAN

Vladivostok

HONSHŪ

Inkutsk

Harbin

Sea
of
Japan

TOKYO

Ulan Bator

NORTH
KOREA

JAPAN

PACIFIC
OCEAN

ALTAI

SHENYANG

MTS.

M O N G O L I A

SEOUL
SOUTH
KOREA

Ürümqi

GOBI (DESERT)

BEIJING

30°

Yellow
Sea

KYŪSHŪ

MAKAN

90°

C   H   I   N   A

Huang

Zhengzhou

120°   SHANGHAI

KUNLUN   SHAN

0	100	200	400	600	800 Miles

0	150	300	600	900	1200 Kilometers

Northern Asia: Industry in a Vast Wilderness

Lake Baikal holds more water than any other lake in the world. It is five thousand feet deep. Its waters are home to hundreds of kinds of plants and animals. The Lake Baikal seal and several species of fish are found here and nowhere else in the world.

The beauty of Lake Baikal and the purity of its clear waters have made it a symbol of nature to the people of the Soviet Union. Thirty years ago, two cellulose mills were built on the lakeshore. Waste from the mills poured into Lake Baikal.

Soon, people in the neighboring communities began to protest because they hated to see the pure lake water harmed by pollution. They formed organizations to protect the lake. The battle to save Lake Baikal was long and hard, but in the end, the people won. Treatment facilities were installed to keep the waste out of the lake.

Lake Baikal is still threatened by other industries on the rivers that flow into it. But the people are continuing their fight, and perhaps the leaders of government and business will also recognize the importance of saving this unique body of water, Lake Baikal.

Another northern Asian body of water, the Aral Sea is threatened by pollution and by the removal of water for irrigation. These will be hard problems to solve. The farmers need the irrigation water and the fishermen need a healthy Aral Sea.

Boats lie on dry land that used to be the bed of the Aral Sea. Removing water for irrigation of the surrounding cultivated lands has shrunk the sea to a fraction of its former size.

How Can We Help?

- By encouraging careful development of this fragile land so that the mistakes made elsewhere in the world will not be repeated.

- By supporting the efforts of the people of the Soviet Union to protect Lake Baikal from industrial pollution.

The beauty of Lake Baikal, the deepest lake in the world, has inspired the people of the Soviet Union to search for ways to protect its waters from pollution.

1960 shoreline

1989 shoreline

estimated shoreline 2000

Aral Sea

This map shows how much the Aral Sea is shrinking. Unless a way is found to let more water into the sea, nothing but small ponds will remain.

Southern Asia: Environments

Southern Asia has the world's highest mountains, the Himalayas. It has vast deserts, mighty rivers, and some of the world's richest rain forests. It also has more of the world's people than any other region.

Most of these people live in small villages rather than in cities. Some are farmers who own their own land. But millions have no land of their own. They survive by working for others or by planting crops on small patches of unclaimed land.

In many Asian countries, there are serious conflicts about the best way to use the land. How much should be used for coffee, tea, and other export crops? How much should be used for growing food? Export crops bring in money to buy machinery and other industrial goods. But many Asians do not have enough to eat. They need the food the land could provide.

Asia is also losing its forests. Tropical wood such as teak brings high prices in industrial countries. Cutting the forests destroys the homes of many kinds of plants and animals.

Above, left: The lush rain forest on the island of Borneo is but one of the natural scenes in the varied landscape of southern Asia.

Above, right: Terraces cut in hillsides are a traditional way to increase available farmland in densely populated southern Asia. These terraces in Nepal also help prevent erosion.

©1991 Rand McNally & Co.

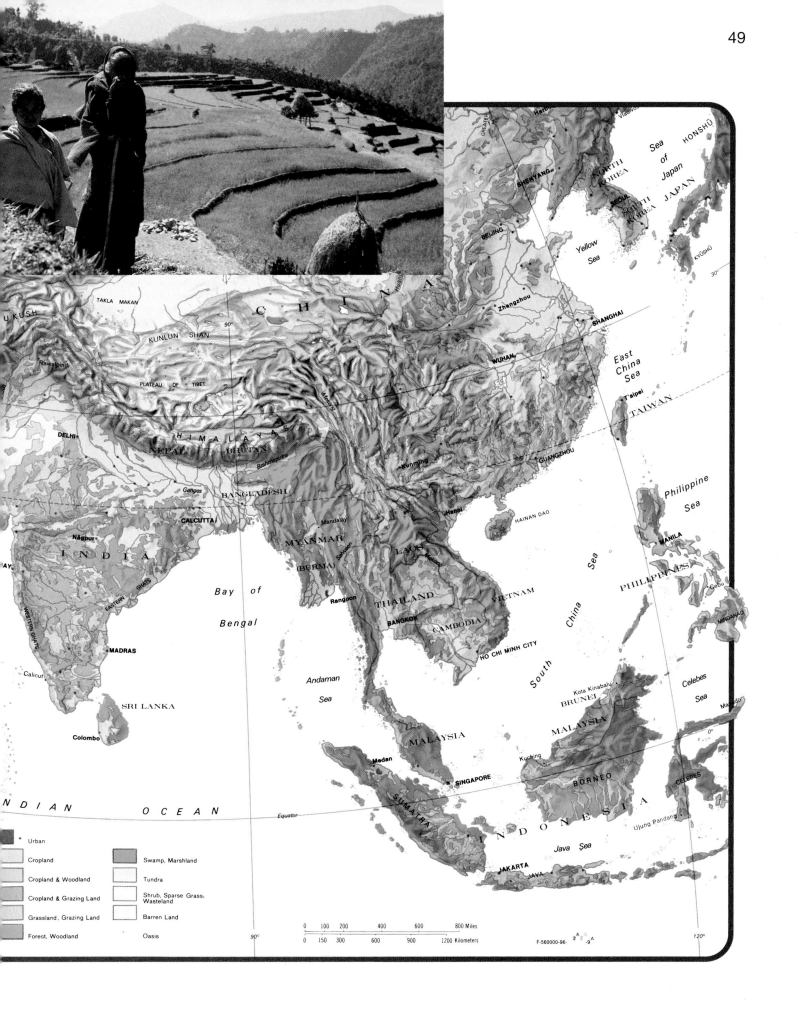

TAKLA MAKAN

U KUSH

KUNLUN SHAN

90°

C H I N A

Harbin 120°

Vladivostok

SHENYANG

NORTH KOREA

Sea of Japan

HONSHŪ

GREATER

SEOUL

SOUTH KOREA

JAPAN

BEIJING

KYŪSHŪ

30°

Huang

Zhengzhou

Yellow Sea

Rawalpindi

PLATEAU OF TIBET

WUHAN

SHANGHAI

East China Sea

Mekong

HIMALAYAS

DELHI

NEPAL

BHUTAN

T'aipei

TAIWAN

Brahmaputra

Kunming

GUANGZHOU

Ganges

BANGLADESH

Hanoi

HAINAN DAO

Philippine Sea

CALCUTTA

Nāgpur

Mandalay

MYANMAR (BURMA)

LAOS

MANILA

I N D I A

Salween

South China Sea

PHILIPPINES

Cebu

EASTERN GHATS

WESTERN GHATS

Bay of Bengal

Rangoon

THAILAND

VIETNAM

MINDANAO

MADRAS

BANGKOK

CAMBODIA

Mekong

Calicut

Andaman Sea

HO CHI MINH CITY

Kota Kinabalu

Celebes Sea

SRI LANKA

BRUNEI

Manado

Colombo

MALAYSIA

MALAYSIA

CELEBES

Kuching

BORNEO

Medan

SINGAPORE

0°

N D I A N   O C E A N

Equator

SUMATRA

I N D O N E S I A

Ujung Pandang

JAKARTA

JAVA

Java Sea

* Urban

Cropland

Cropland & Woodland

Cropland & Grazing Land

Grassland, Grazing Land

Forest, Woodland

Swamp, Marshland

Tundra

Shrub, Sparse Grass, Wasteland

Barren Land

Oasis

0	100	200	400	600	800 Miles
0	150	300	600	900	1200 Kilometers

90°

F-560000-96

-9

120°

Southern Asia: Protecting the Soil

Southern Asia loses 25 billion tons of soil through erosion every year. The rate of erosion is 25 times higher than in the United States. *Deforestation* is the biggest single cause of this erosion. Trees are being cut from steep slopes. They are cut for timber and for firewood. Some are cut by poor farmers needing the land to grow food.

On slopes covered with trees, roots hold the rain. The water sinks into the soil. But when the trees are cut, the water runs downhill, carrying the soil with it. On slopes with no trees, the rainfall quickly flows off the land into the rivers. This causes floods. On forested slopes, the soil soaks up water when it rains and lets it go gradually when it is dry. The rivers flow more evenly all year-round, so even in the dry season, there is enough water for irrigation.

India, China, and Nepal all have large *reforestation* efforts. India has been planting over three million acres of trees each year, but it is still losing forest because many trees are cut for fuel, for building materials, and to make room for cropland needed to feed the nation's large population. To protect the soil, more effective ways to cook, build, and farm must be developed. For example, solar cookers and more efficient stoves are ways to cut back on the use of firewood for cooking. And bricks for buildings can replace much of the demand for wood. Ways to feed people without depleting forested slopes must be found.

Rain falls on bare hillsides after forests have been cut. There are no roots to hold the water. It rushes downhill, carrying the soil with it. The muddy rivers overflow when so much water enters all at once. In dry seasons, no water enters the river. Many of southern Asia's larger rivers now flood every year during the rainy season and dry up when no rains fall. Forests hold the water and release it gradually, so floods are less common and the rivers flow all year.

How Can We Help?

- By encouraging reforestation work in the nations of southern Asia.

- By continuing to look for ways to grow more food on less land so that the people of southern Asia can grow what they need without clearing more forest land.

- By looking for ways to reduce the need for wood as a fuel for cooking and other needs.

Above: The people of southern Asia, with help from their governments and from private organizations, are planting millions of trees every year. The trees will protect the soil and provide fuel and wood for the future.

Left: On the island of Mindanao in the Philippines, all the trees have been cut from a steep hillside. Heavy rains will soon erode the soil from this clear-cut land.

Africa: Environments

The plains of East Africa were the first home of humanity. It was there that humans first began to use tools. It was from there that they began to spread over the entire earth.

In much of Africa, the climate is dry. Rain falls during only a few months every year, and in some years, the rains do not come at all. The dry climate and poor soils make agriculture difficult in most of Africa.

The driest region is the Sahara Desert. The largest desert in the world, it covers most of the northern third of the continent. Few people can live on this dry land. South of the desert, the average rainfall increases. Grassland and *savanna* replace the bare sands of the desert. Savannas are grasslands dotted with widely scattered trees. Most of Africa's famous large animals live on the savanna.

The wettest parts of the continent are along the Atlantic Coast south of the desert and in the Congo River Basin. Much of this land is dominated by tropical rain forest. The richest of these forests is in the Congo River Basin.

Most of Africa's people live in the country rather than the city. This small village in the nation of Zimbabwe is one of thousands of small communities on the continent.

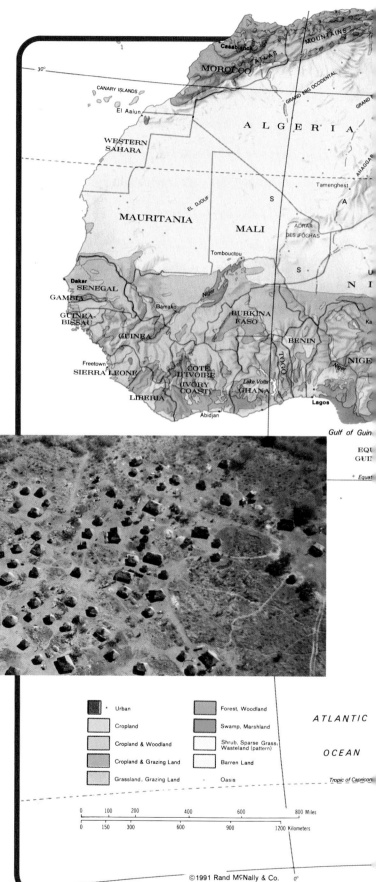

Urban

Cropland

Cropland & Woodland

Cropland & Grazing Land

Grassland, Grazing Land

Forest, Woodland

Swamp, Marshland

Shrub, Sparse Grass, Wasteland (pattern)

Barren Land

Oasis

© 1991 Rand McNally & Co.

| 0 | 100 | 200 | 400 | 600 | 800 Miles |
| 0 | 150 | 300 | 600 | 900 | 1200 Kilometers |

Wilderness areas in every corner of the world are home to animals as well as plants. Africa is especially rich in its array of large wild animals. Here zebra and wildebeest herds gather at a water hole in a game preserve in Kenya.

Africa: Garden or Desert?

We call it *desertification*. Expected rains do not fall. Land where the sweet grass fed herds of cattle turns into bare sand. Sand dunes cover croplands. When we misuse the land by heavy grazing or plowing, we make desertification worse. Water vapor rises from land covered with grass or trees. It forms clouds and falls as rain. Water vapor does not rise from earth laid bare by plowing or heavy grazing.

Drought began to feed desertification twenty years ago along the southern edge of the Sahara Desert. Many people starved when their crops failed. Now, individual countries, regional organizations, private development agencies, and the United Nations are working with the local people to try to stop—and even reverse—the advance of the desert.

The Greenbelt Movement in Kenya has inspired women in rural villages to plant millions of young trees. Rangeland-management schemes seek ways to use grasslands for grazing without destroying them. *Agroforestry* is a way to grow crops in narrow strips between rows of trees that shelter the soil. These efforts point toward ways to live on the land without destroying it.

Agroforestry projects, like this one in Niger, can reclaim desertified land. Shelter belts of trees protect crops of millet from desert wind and heat. The trees also provide fuel and help enrich the soil.

Without rain, he cannot plant a crop, but this farmer in Senegal works with his team of oxen to keep them in practice. If rains come, his animals will be ready to help him grow food.

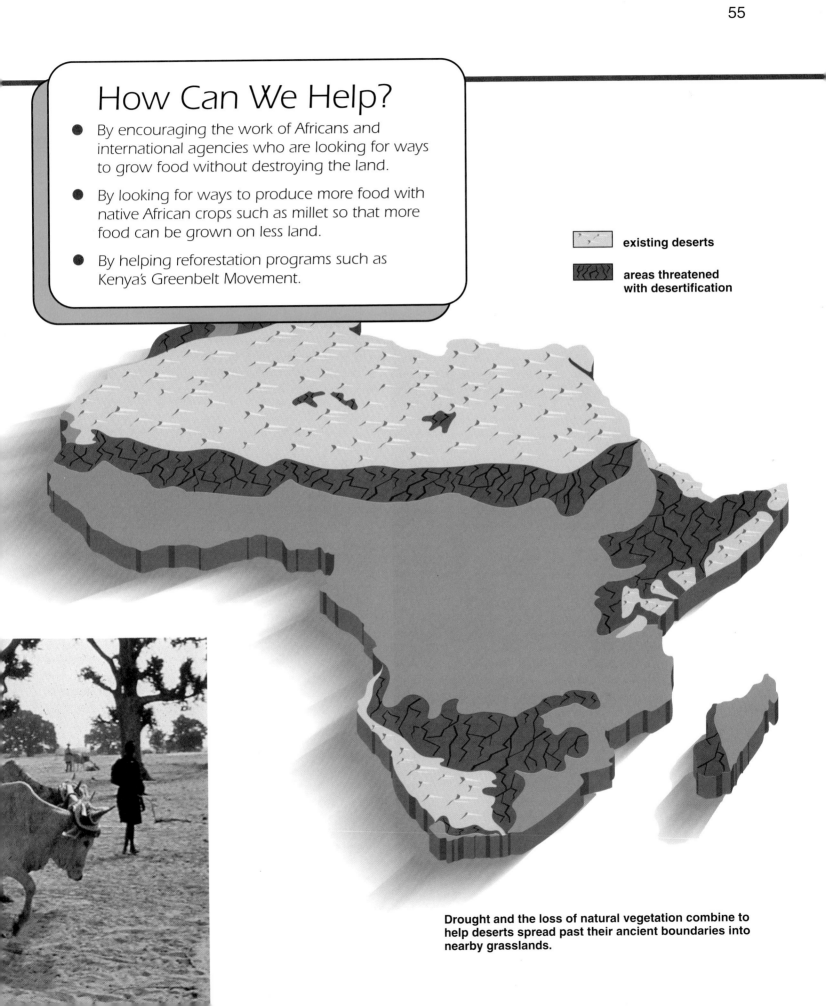

How Can We Help?

- By encouraging the work of Africans and international agencies who are looking for ways to grow food without destroying the land.

- By looking for ways to produce more food with native African crops such as millet so that more food can be grown on less land.

- By helping reforestation programs such as Kenya's Greenbelt Movement.

existing deserts

areas threatened with desertification

Drought and the loss of natural vegetation combine to help deserts spread past their ancient boundaries into nearby grasslands.

Oceania: Environments

Isolated is the best word to describe Australia and the other islands of the South Pacific. Australia is home to kangaroos, koalas, wombats, platypuses, and other animals found nowhere else on earth. Yet cats, hoofed animals, and many other familiar groups were never able to reach the island continent.

The Pacific islands were the last places on earth to be inhabited by people. The first humans did not arrive in New Zealand until A.D. 800. Regular contact between these islands and the rest of the world did not start until about two hundred years ago.

Since that time, Europeans and Asians have emigrated in large numbers to Australia and New Zealand. Polynesians and other groups who arrived before Europeans make up most of the populations of the smaller islands.

Most of Australia is very dry. Nearly all the people live near the coast. There are some small areas of rain forest in the north. New Zealand's native vegetation was mostly forest. Much of it has been cleared now for pasture. Most of the smaller Pacific islands were covered with a rich tropical forest. Large areas have been cut in recent years.

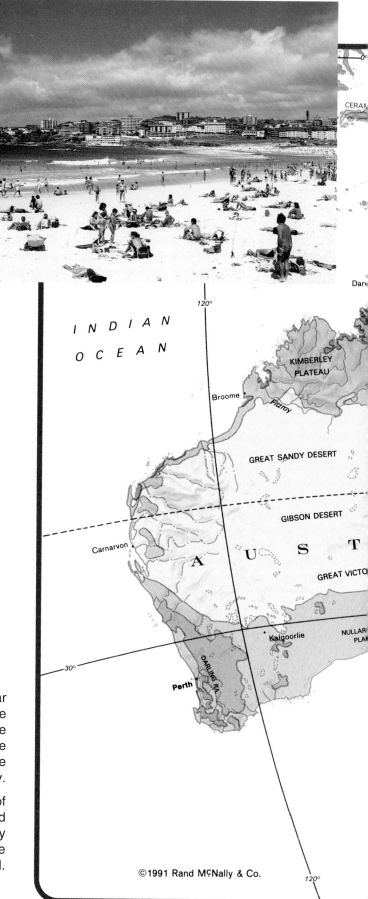

Above, left: Most Australians live near the ocean, especially in the southeastern part of the country. Here rainfall is higher and the climate more tolerable to humans. Shown here is the large city of Sydney.

Above, right: Much of the interior of Australia is desert, or near desert, and is largely uninhabited. The low, scrubby vegetation here in a national park in the Northern Territory is typical.

©1991 Rand McNally & Co.

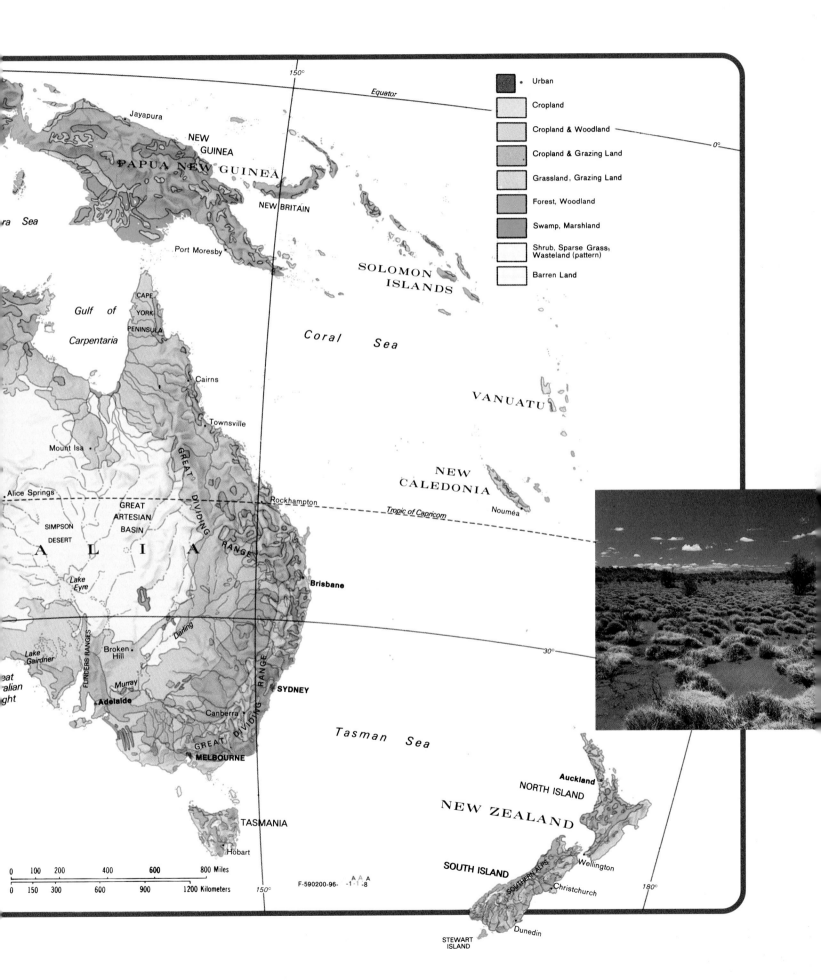

Equator

150°

0°

30°

180°

Urban

Cropland

Cropland & Woodland

Cropland & Grazing Land

Grassland, Grazing Land

Forest, Woodland

Swamp, Marshland

**Shrub, Sparse Grass,
Wasteland (pattern)**

Barren Land

Jayapura

NEW
GUINEA

PAPUA NEW GUINEA

NEW BRITAIN

Port Moresby

CAPE
YORK
PENINSULA

Gulf   of

Carpentaria

ra Sea

SOLOMON
ISLANDS

Coral   Sea

VANUATU

NEW
CALEDONIA

Nouméa

Cairns

Townsville

Mount Isa

Alice Springs

GREAT
ARTESIAN
BASIN

SIMPSON
DESERT

A   L   I   A

Lake
Eyre

Rockhampton

Tropic of Capricorn

Brisbane

GREAT DIVIDING RANGE

Darling

Broken
Hill

Lake
Gairdner

FLINDERS RANGES

Murray

Adelaide

Canberra

SYDNEY

eat
alian
ght

reat

GREAT DIVIDING RANGE

MELBOURNE

Tasman   Sea

TASMANIA

Hobart

Auckland

NORTH ISLAND

NEW ZEALAND

SOUTH ISLAND

SOUTHERN ALPS

Wellington

Christchurch

Dunedin

STEWART
ISLAND

0	100	200	400		600		800 Miles
0	150	300	600		900		1200 Kilometers

150°

F-590200-96- -1-1-8

A A A

Oceania: Leaving Nature Alone

When Englishmen began to settle in New Zealand in the nineteenth century, it seemed a strange place. It had none of the familiar animals of home. The only mammals were bats. Many of the birds had no wings. So the English imported rabbits and deer to hunt. They brought in their favorite song birds. Most of the new species died out. But others spread and multiplied. In fact, the rabbits and deer became terrible pests.

So the people imported weasels, ferrets, and stoats— predators who ate rabbits. But the new predators started to eat the birds that could not fly. The birds had never seen a predator and had no way to defend themselves. Seventeen species of birds have vanished. Others survive only on offshore islands where the imported predators have not reached.

Government wildlife managers have moved kiwis and kakapos— the world's only flightless parrots—to these island refuges. Only about sixty kakapos are left alive. New Zealanders are making heroic efforts to save them, but they may be too late.

The story is the same on many other islands. Australia lost eighteen species of mammals. There are now strict laws against importing animals. Maybe we are learning to love nature as it is. When we try to rearrange it, we often destroy it.

Cat

Laughing Owl

Short-tailed Bat

Common Rabbit

The animals shown with the arrows have been imported into New Zealand in the past two centuries. They have driven the other animals shown either to extinction or nearly to extinction by competing with them for food or by eating them.

How Can We Help?

- By insisting on strict controls to prevent people from moving wild animals from one land to another.

- By supporting the efforts of the countries of Oceania to protect their remaining native species from the harm done by imported species.

Weasel

Kakapo

Canada Goose

Red Deer

Ferret

Top: The brown kiwi, a symbol of the nation of New Zealand, is one of many native birds threatened with extinction because of environmental changes.

Bottom: The tuatara, the only survivor of an ancient family of reptiles, lives only in New Zealand. It survives on small off-shore islands that have not been colonized by animals introduced to New Zealand in recent years.

North America: Environments

North America is variety. It is tropical rain forests in Panama and Nicaragua. It is hot deserts in northern Mexico and the southwestern United States. It is broad prairies in the central United States and Canada. It is temperate zone rain forest in Oregon, Washington, and British Columbia. It is tundra where the soil is frozen year-round in the Northwest Territories and Alaska. It is New York City and Mexico City, two of the largest urban areas on earth.

Industry came to North America in the cities of the northeastern United States. It then spread to the southern and western states. In Canada, the province of Ontario has most of the nation's industry. In Mexico, Mexico City and the cities of the north have much new industry.

The prairies at the heart of the continent are mainly cropland. Half of the world's corn and almost one-third of its wheat grow on this land. In the southwestern United States and northern Mexico, irrigation has turned deserts into rich farmland. Fruits and vegetables can be grown year-round in the warm climate.

The United States and Canada are among the world's richest countries. The southern part of the continent, southern Mexico and Central America, is still quite poor. Most of the people live in rural areas. Many have no land.

- Urban
- Cropland
- Cropland & Woodland
- Cropland & Grazing Land
- Grassland, Grazing Land
- Forest, Woodland
- Swamp, Marshland
- Tundra
- Shrub, Sparse Grass, Wasteland
- Barren Land

| 0 | 100 | 200 | 400 | 600 | 800 Miles |

| 0 | 150 | 300 | 600 | 900 | 1200 Kilometers |

©1991 Rand McNally & Co.

F-520000-9

Above: Snow-capped Mt. Moran overlooks a bend in the Snake River in Wyoming's Grand Teton National Park. Most of North America's remaining wilderness is in protected parks and preserves.

Left: The huge circles of green in these barley and potato fields in Colorado are made by irrigation machines that move in circles around a central water source.

North America: Cleaning Up

Above: Hazardous wastes carelessly dumped in steel drums are a disaster waiting to happen. As the barrels rust, they begin to leak, spreading poisons into the air, ground, and water.

Left: A crew begins work on an abandoned toxic-waste dump. Thousands of such dumps need to be cleaned up to prevent the spread of toxic wastes.

American industry has invented thousands of new products: fabrics like nylon, plastics that can be used for everything from car seats to soft-drink bottles. Some of these products—like *asbestos* insulation or the chemicals called *PCBs*—are harmful to people. In other cases, dangerous waste products were left over after products were manufactured.

For many years, there were very few controls on disposal of hazardous wastes. Some were just poured into the nearest river. Others were placed in steel drums and buried. Often, people did not realize that they were creating a danger to the environment by dumping these wastes.

Now that we have begun to understand, we have passed laws against such dumping. Industries must now get a government permit to use hazardous materials. They cannot get a permit unless they have a plan for proper disposal of wastes.

But we are still left with the job of cleaning up after almost 100 years of careless dumping. In 1980, the United States Congress created the Superfund Program to clean up these dumps. More than 1,200 dumps sites have been identified so far. More than 300 of these had been cleaned up by late 1990, and work had begun on many of the others.

How Can We Help?

- By supporting Superfund and other programs that clean up dangerous waste dumps.

- By encouraging careful control of toxic wastes produced by today's industries so we will not have new dumps to worry about in the future.

- By looking for ways to produce the goods we need without creating toxic wastes.

The dots on the map show the locations of major toxic-waste dumps in the United States. The wastes in many of these dumps were produced years ago, long before there were any controls on dumping. Some of these dumps are leaking poisons into streams or ground water. The U.S. government has begun a major effort to find and clean up all these old dumps.

○ **major toxic-waste site**

North America: Energy Use or Abuse?

North America has only 8 percent of the world's people, but those 8 percent use almost 30 percent of the world's energy. But as energy costs climb and pollution from burning oil and coal gets worse, North Americans are changing their habits. They are looking for ways to conserve energy and ways to get more energy from sources that do not harm the environment.

Many cities are setting aside special lanes on freeways for buses and carpools. The promise of a faster trip should encourage more people to use these energy-efficient ways to commute. In Los Angeles, California, and other cities, new rail systems carry commuters more efficiently than cars.

A solar thermal power plant in the Mojave Desert is turning sunlight into electricity at a cost 25 percent less than electricity from nuclear power plants. This kind of solar power plant could supply 35 percent of U.S. electricity.

Recycling is a big energy saver. It takes far less energy to make aluminum cans from old cans than from raw ore. Half the cans used in the United States are now recycled, and many cities are starting large recycling programs to increase that amount.

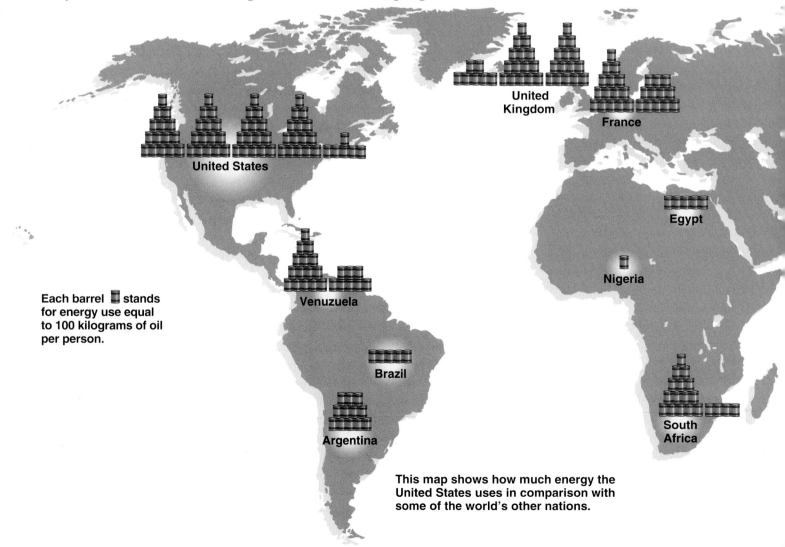

United Kingdom

France

United States

Egypt

Venezuela

Nigeria

Each barrel stands for energy use equal to 100 kilograms of oil per person.

Brazil

South Africa

Argentina

This map shows how much energy the United States uses in comparison with some of the world's other nations.

Below: This school was designed to be heated by the sun. Panels that collect solar heat are used on many buildings today to save on heating costs.

Above: Nearly all the cars on this freeway are carrying just one person. Americans use large amounts of energy just getting to work and back. Using car pools, buses, and trains leads to big energy savings.

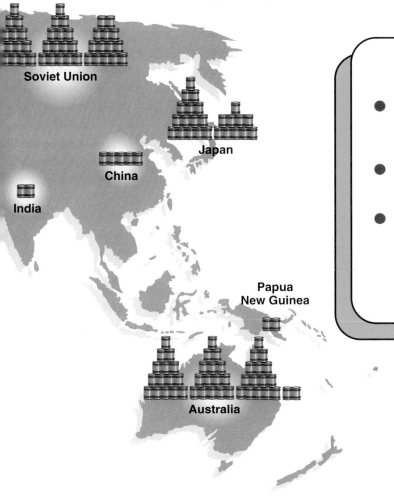

Soviet Union

Japan

China

India

Papua New Guinea

Australia

How Can We Help?

- By building cars that get better gas mileage. And by using public transportation or car pools whenever possible.

- By insulating our homes and using more efficient refrigerators, water heaters, and other appliances.

- By encouraging research into ways to conserve energy in business and industry. And by encouraging research into solar power, wind power, and other renewable and nonpolluting energy sources.

South America: Environments

The Andes Mountains form a long chain along the west coast of South America. Some of the peaks are so high they are covered with snow even at the equator. East of the mountains, the northern and southern ends of the continent are broad grasslands. At the heart of South America is the great Amazon River Basin, home of the largest system of rivers and the largest tropical forest in the world.

The people of South America are a mixture of native peoples of the continent, Europeans—especially Spaniards and Portuguese—and Africans. Until recently, most of South America's people lived in cities, or along the coasts, or in regions with rich soil or minerals. Much of the continent, especially the Amazon River Basin, was wilderness inhabited by relatively small numbers of people who had little contact with the rest of the world.

That is now changing. The countries of South America are developing large portions of their lands. The grasslands of Argentina, called *pampas*, are being turned into wheat fields. Highland forests are becoming coffee plantations. Tropical forests are giving way to cattle ranches, highways, dams, and mines.

Lake Titicaca lies on the border of Peru and Bolivia, high in the Andes. People have lived on its shores for thousands of years. Here a fisherman casts his net in the icy waters.

These peaks in Argentina are typical of the rugged landscape of the Andes Mountains. The flat lands in the foreground support grazing animals such as the guanaco.

Barranquilla
CARACAS
Port of Spain
TRINIDAD
Panamá
LLANOS
Orinoco
VENEZUELA
GUYANA
Georgetown
ATLANTIC
BOGOTÁ
COLOMBIA
SURINAME
FRENCH
GUIANA
OCEAN
Quito
ECUADOR
Negro
Equator
0°
0°
Belém
Amazon
Manaus
Iquitos
SELVAS
Fortaleza
B R A Z I L
PERU
Rio Branco
São Francisco
Recife
LIMA
ANDES
Salvador
PACIFIC
BOLIVIA
Cuiabá
La Paz
MATO
Brasília
GROSSO
OCEAN
CHACO
Belo Horizonte
Iquique
Paraná
SÃO PAULO
RIO DE JANEIRO
Tropic of Capricorn
PARAGUAY
Asunción
San Miguel de Tucumán
30°
30°
Porto Alegre
Córdoba
URUGUAY
SANTIAGO
BUENOS AIRES
Montevideo
PAMPA
CHILE
Bahía Blanca
ARGENTINA
ATLANTIC
Puerto Montt
PATAGONIA
OCEAN

Urban
Cropland
Cropland & Woodland
Cropland & Grazing Land
Grassland, Grazing Land
Forest, Woodland
Swamp, Marshland
Shrub, Sparse Grass, Wasteland
Barren Land

| 0 | 100 | 200 | 400 | 600 | 800 Miles |
| 0 | 150 | 300 | 600 | 900 | 1200 Kilometers |

©1991 Rand McNally & Co.

F-540000-96-
60°
FALKLAND ISLANDS
30°
Punta Arenas
TIERRA
DEL FUEGO

South America: Preserving the Hidden Places

Explorers in the Amazon are still finding groups of Indians who have never had any contact with the outside world. They live in forests so huge that no outsider has ever penetrated them. But now even the vast forests of the Amazon are falling. Every year, thousands of square miles of forest are cut and burned.

Sometimes the forests are replaced by cattle ranches, sometimes by small farms. The ranches and farms usually don't succeed. Rain forest soils do not hold the minerals needed to grow grass or crops. But so many people need land that they are always willing to keep trying farms deeper in the forest.

These forests are home to millions of kinds of plants and animals. Some of these are going extinct as their homes are cut and burned. In Brazil, Indians and other forest dwellers are trying to put a stop to the destruction. They have lived in the forests for centuries. They have a deep knowledge of the plants and animals. They know ways to earn a living from the forest without destroying it. They are now working with scientists from outside the Amazon to give their knowledge to other people.

Above: A dense carpet of tree seedlings begins growing in preparation for a reforestation project. Research looks for ways to reforest areas that have been cut or burned.

Left: Rain quickly carves deep gulleys in tropical forest soils when the trees are cut. Few plants can grow on this eroded soil.

How Can We Help?

- By setting aside parks and preserves where the rain forest can be protected from development.

- By searching for ways to use the rain forest without destroying it. From resources in the rain forest, we can produce food and medicinal plants, rubber, fish, and other useful things.

Fires set to clear trees from land may burn out of control and destroy valuable forests not scheduled for clearing.

Wasteful logging methods destroy more trees than they harvest and leave forest animals with no habitat.

Most farms on land carved from the rain forest fail after a few crops have been harvested.

Cattle ranches have been started on cleared forest land, but forest soils are not rich and most ranches fail within a few years.

Polar Regions: Environments

The North Pole is in the Arctic Ocean where the water reaches a depth of fifteen thousand feet. People have lived on the land surrounding the Arctic Ocean for thousands of years. This northern region has many birds and mammals. The South Pole is in the middle of Antarctica, a continent where the land is buried under ice thousands of feet thick. Antarctica is the only continent with no permanent human settlements. There are no land animals in this southern region. They are different in many ways, but the regions around the earth's poles are in other ways very much alike. They are both very cold. They are both dark for half the year.

The cold and darkness mean that the polar regions receive little solar energy. They cannot support the richness of life found in tropical forests. There are large herds of reindeer in the Arctic, but they must wander over thousands of square miles of tundra to find enough to eat. Most of the birds of the Arctic live there only in summer. They fly south to escape the cold, dark winters.

The seas are richer, especially in the Antarctic. There, tiny shrimplike creatures called *krill* are food for penguins, other seabirds, and whales.

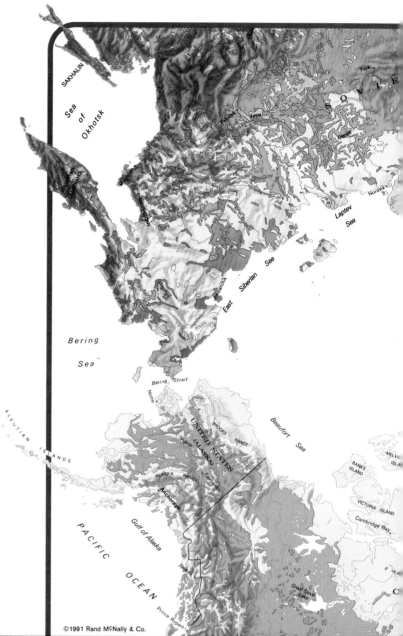

©1991 Rand McNally & Co.

Near right: Penguins are part of the natural environment of Antarctica and the surrounding waters and islands. Development in Antarctica could damage their nesting and feeding areas.

Far right: Research bases like this one are among the few permanent human settlements on the cold and barren continent of Antarctica.

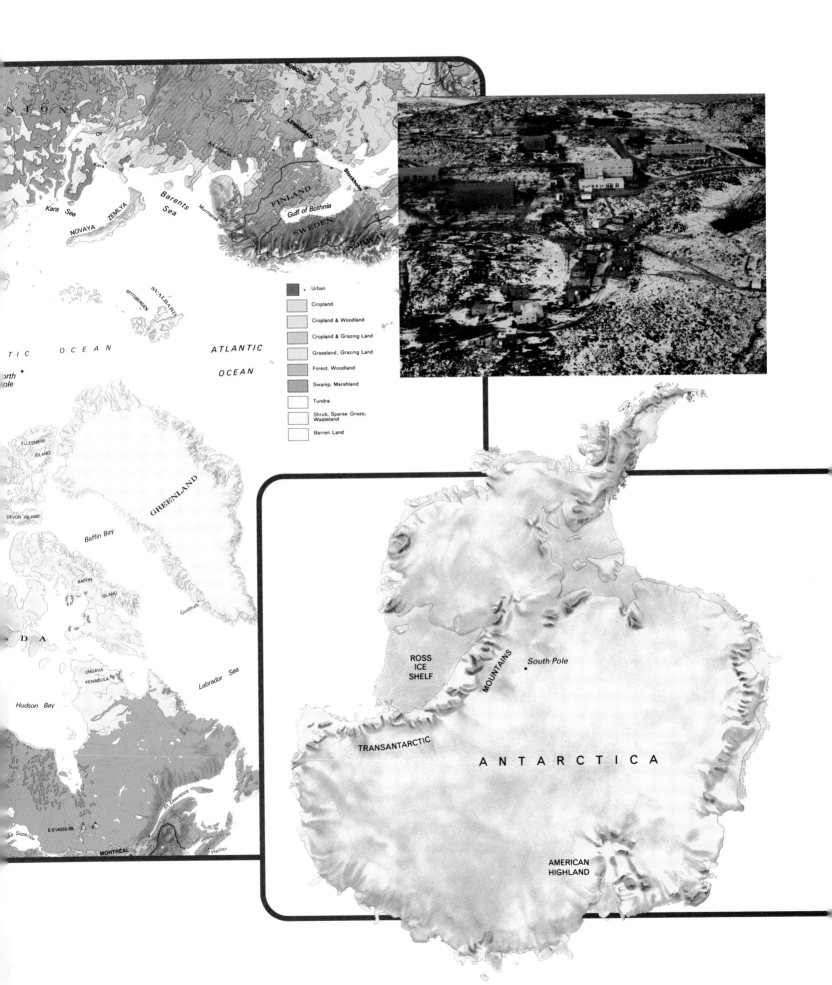

71

Moscow

Sukhona

Dnepr

LENINGRAD

Ob

Arkhangelsk

Kara

FINLAND

Stockholm

Kara Sea

Barents Sea

Gulf of Bothnia

NOVAYA ZEMLYA

Murmansk

SWEDEN

NORWAY

SVALBARD

SPITSBERGEN

ARCTIC OCEAN

ATLANTIC OCEAN

North Pole

ATLANTIC OCEAN

Urban

Cropland

Cropland & Woodland

Cropland & Grazing Land

Grassland, Grazing Land

Forest, Woodland

Swamp, Marshland

Tundra

Shrub, Sparse Grass, Wasteland

Barren Land

ELLESMERE ISLAND

DEVON ISLAND

GREENLAND

Baffin Bay

Godthab

BAFFIN ISLAND

CANADA

Hudson Bay

UNGAVA PENINSULA

Labrador Sea

Lake Superior

E-514000-96

MONTREAL

St. Lawrence

Halifax

ROSS ICE SHELF

MOUNTAINS

South Pole

TRANSANTARCTIC

A N T A R C T I C A

AMERICAN HIGHLAND

Polar Regions: Protecting the Fragile Wilderness

The oil fields at Prudhoe Bay in Alaska produce as much nitrogen oxide, a chemical that contributes to make smog, as all of Washington, D.C. Sulfur emissions from the Soviet mines on the Kola Peninsula near the city of Murmansk are twice as high as the emissions from all the industry in Finland. Rain is rare in the Arctic, so these pollutants stay in the air. They make "Arctic haze," a smog that is often as dense as the smog that hangs over Los Angeles.

The polar regions are delicate places. Things grow and change so slowly that damage remains for many years. Tire tracks on the tundra may still be visible fifty years after they were laid down. The polar regions are also very rich in vital resources such as oil, iron, titanium, chromium, gold, and other minerals.

The eight countries with land in the Arctic met together for the first time in 1989 to begin working on ways to protect their northern possessions. Twenty-nine countries have signed a protection agreement on Antarctica. These actions are only a beginning, but they could point the way toward protection for our fragile polar lands and waters.

Above: In the cold, dry climate of Antarctica, garbage lasts almost forever. The trash left behind at this abandoned research base will be clearly visible a century from now.

Right: The Lapps of northern Scandinavia depend on their herds of reindeer for food and clothing. Their animals have helped them live on the bleak Arctic tundra without destroying the land.

How Can We Help?

- By encouraging cooperation between countries to find ways to protect the fragile poles from damage.

- By setting aside preserves to protect the unique wildlife of the polar regions.

- By using the long experience and rich knowledge of the peoples of the Arctic as a guide to living in these cold regions.

Recent exploration has shown that Antarctica, the frozen continent, may be rich in minerals. The world must choose whether to risk serious damage to this wilderness in pursuit of the mineral wealth. This map shows some of the major deposits on Antarctica.

Mineral deposits

Coal deposits

Possible gas and oil deposits

Glossary

Acid rain   Rain (or snow) that has gained a large acid content by falling through air pollutants.

Agroforestry   A farming method that plants crops in narrow strips between rows of trees. The trees shelter the crops from heat, wind, and dryness.

Algae   Simple green plants that mostly live in water.

Antarctic Circle   The line of latitude 66.5 degrees south of the equator. South of the Antarctic Circle the sun does not rise in the winter or set in the summer.

Arctic Circle   The line of latitude 66.5 degrees north of the equator. North of the Arctic Circle the sun does not rise in the winter or set in the summer.

Arctic haze   A kind of *smog* caused by air pollution in Arctic regions.

Asbestos   A mineral once widely used as insulation. It has been discovered to cause lung cancer.

Biome   One of the earth's major living communities— for example, rain forest, grassland, desert, tundra.

Biosphere   The home of all the earth's living things, it extends from the bottom of the deepest ocean to the lower levels of the atmosphere.

Carbon dioxide (CO$_2$)   A gas formed of a combination of one atom of carbon and two atoms of oxygen. An important part of the atmosphere.

Chlorofluorocarbons (CFCs) Humanmade gases combining chlorine, fluorine, and carbon. Widely used in refrigerators and air conditioners, they contribute to *ozone* destruction and to the *greenhouse effect*.

Chlorophyll   The green pigment that allows plants to make food from sunlight.

Climate   The weather conditions in an area over a long period of time.

Contour plowing   Plowing farm fields across slopes, instead of up and down them, to prevent *erosion*.

Coriolis effect   An effect of the rotation of the earth that causes air and water to move in spirals rather than straight lines.

DDT   A pesticide used to kill insects. It has been found to do harm to other animals as well.

Deforestation   Clearing of forests by cutting or burning.

Desertification   The process that converts grasslands or woodlands to desert.

Developing country   A country where the people work mainly at farming, mining, or logging but not in industry.

Drought   A long dry period when no rain falls.

Emission   A substance given off into air or water.

Endangered species   A kind of plant or animal whose population has become so small it is in danger of *extinction*.

Energy cycle   The movement of energy from the sun through living things.

Erosion   The wearing away of a substance. Soil is worn away by water and wind.

Export crop   Crops grown to be sold to other countries rather than used by the people who grow them.

Extinct   No longer existing. A species of plant or animal becomes extinct when no members of the species are left alive.

Fertility   A measure of the ability of soil to grow plants. Fertile soils are rich in the minerals plants need.

Fertilizer   Subtances containing essential minerals which are added to soils to increase fertility.

Gamma rays   A form of radiation of very high energy. Exposure to gamma rays is very harmful to living things.

Glaciers   Moving ice deposits.

Glucose   A simple form of sugar made by plants from sunlight.

Greenhouse effect   The holding of heat from the sun by the atmosphere. If we change the atmosphere so it can hold more heat, the earth's climate will become warmer.

Ground water   Water held in pores in rock under the earth's surface. Pumped from wells, it is a major source of drinking water for people.

Habitat The kind of place a plant or animal normally lives in.

Hazardous wastes Dangerous substances left over from manufacturing. They may be poisonous, explosive, or capable of causing disease.

Hydrologic cycle The movement of water from oceans to clouds to the earth—as rain or snow—and then through rivers back to the ocean.

Industrial country A nation where most of the people work in manufacturing or service jobs rather than farming.

Irrigate To carry water from wells or rivers to crops. Irrigation allows us to have farms in areas with little rainfall.

Krill Tiny creatures similar to shrimp, which live in the Antarctic Ocean and provide food for penguins, whales, and seabirds.

Mangrove A small tree that grows in tangled thickets on the shores of tropical seas.

Millet A grain that is an important food crop in Africa.

Nitric acid A corrosive compound made of nitrogen, oxygen, and hydrogen. It is a compound in *acid rain*.

Nitrogen oxide A compound given off by burning oil or gasoline that is converted to *nitric acid* in the air.

Northern Hemisphere The part of the earth north of the equator.

Organic farming Farming without the use of chemical *fertilizers*.

Oxygen An important gas in the earth's atmosphere.

Ozone layer A part of the atmosphere more than ten miles up where a special form of oxygen called *ozone* is common. Ozone protects the earth from *ultraviolet rays*.

PCBs Compounds once used in various industrial processes. They have been found to be very harmful to living things.

Pesticides Chemicals used to kill insects, weeds, and other living things that attack crops.

Plates The name given to the huge slabs of rock that form the earth's crust.

Pollutant Any substance that contaminates the environment.

Rain forest Forests found where heavy rains fall all or part of the year. Most are in the tropics.

Recycle To recover and reuse resources.

Reforestation To replant forests on land that forests had been taken from.

Savanna A region where the major vegetation is grasses and scattered trees.

Smog Air pollution created by smoke, car exhaust, and industrial fumes.

Solar thermal power A way of generating electricity by using mirrors to concentrate sunlight to boil water to drive steam generators.

Southern Hemisphere That part of the earth south of the equator.

Species A kind of plant or animal. A species consists of populations that can breed with each other.

Sulfur dioxide A compound given off by burning coal or oil.

Sulfuric acid A corrosive acid formed in the air from *sulfur dioxide*. A major part of acid rain.

Taiga The forest of evergreen trees that grows just south of the *tundra* in Eurasia and North America.

Tropics That part of the earth that lies near the equator, between the Tropic of Cancer and the Tropic of Capricorn.

Tundra The community of ground-hugging plants that dominates the land in the Arctic and on high mountains.

Ultraviolet rays Radiation in waves slightly shorter than visible light. It is harmful to living things.

Vegetation The combination of species that creates the typical plant life of a region.

Weather The day-to-day changes in temperature, wind direction, and rainfall.

Wetlands Lands covered all or part of the time by shallow waters.

X-rays Very short wave, high-energy radiation. Very harmful to living things.

Subject Index

Numbers in *italics* refer to illustrations, maps, or photographs.

Index to Major Places on the Maps